MIRACLES
& HEALING
MADE
easy

MIRACLES & HEALING MADE *easy*

INSPIRING STORIES OF FAITH

CARLIE TERRADEZ

4 5 6 7 8 9 / 23 22 21 20 19

Miracles & Healing Made Easy: Inspiring Stories of Faith
ISBN: 978-1-68031-097-9
Copyright © 2016 by Carlie Terradez

Published by Harrison House Publishers

TABLE OF CONTENTS

FOREWORD

Carlie Terradez is the co-leader of Charis Bible College's Healing School. Since 2011, she has led weekly healing schools and trained over 1,000 students to minister healing to those in need.

In 2014, she helped lead our first Healing Is Here conference where we saw over 1,000 people miraculously healed. I've been in a number of the great healing evangelist's meetings and have never seen more miracles in a three-day meeting than I did in those meetings.

Carlie also trains and oversees all the prayer ministers at our Gospel Truth rallies and seminars. We consistently see miracles, including people getting out of wheel chairs, blind eyes opening, hearing being restored, and a multitude of other physical problems being healed.

But it wasn't always this way. Carlie lived with epilepsy and allergies for decades. Her daughter Hannah was on the brink of death at the age of three. Carlie's life could have turned out much differently. But God miraculously intervened. And today,

Carlie and her husband, Ashley, are taking the truths the Lord has taught them and setting people free all over the world.

By Carlie's own admission, she doesn't operate in a special gift of healing. She just takes the truths of God's Word and receives what the Lord has provided for every one of His children.

In this book, Carlie will guide you through her own struggles and help you arrive at the place of healing she has come to enjoy. God wants you well, and Carlie can help you receive what is rightfully yours.

Andrew Wommack

ACKNOWLEDGMENTS

Being my first book, this really has been a long time in the making. I'd like to dedicate it to my long-suffering family: my amazing husband, Ashley, who brought me coffee in bed every morning and caused a delicious aroma of bacon to waft upstairs to me as I typed away on Saturday mornings. To our three children, Zachary, Joshua, and Hannah, whose unadulterated faith, sense of adventure, and tenacity inspire me frequently and challenge me daily! You have demonstrated Jesus to me in more ways than I can explain with words. I love you with all my heart.

There are a number of people throughout my life who have encouraged me and mentored me, but there are two men in particular whom I'd like to thank. Andrew Wommack, you revealed the Gospel to me in a way that I had never heard it, and the truth of God's love changed my perception of Him. Not only did this truth powerfully affect my life, but it spilled out into my family and saved our little girl. Forever, thank you.

Daniel Amstutz, you are a mighty man of God! Thank you for allowing us the opportunity to serve at Charis Bible College Healing School and minister alongside you—so much fun and laughter, and such a privilege to be a part of your team. Seeing lives changed on a weekly basis only proved to me that miracles really are a piece of cake for Jesus!

Love Always,
Carlie

one

MIRACLES START IN THE HEART

Miracles and healing can be controversial subjects in the body of Christ. I know my family's views on the subjects have changed over the years, partly due to our experiences, but predominantly because we heard the Gospel. We were Christians nearly 12 years before we heard the full Gospel message. Though we received salvation through belief in Jesus, we didn't understand that the Gospel is much more than just a ticket to heaven. Romans 1:16 (AMP) calls it the "good news." It is "the power of God unto salvation for all who believe." This literally means the Gospel is the good news of God's miracle working, abundant, mighty power to deliver, heal, save, forgive, and protect from harm all those who trust in Jesus! That is good news!

Understanding this concept gave my family a hunger to see more of God's power play out in our lives. In John 10:10, Jesus said He came to give us life and life more abundantly. We decided to stop settling for *life* when we were promised *abundant life*. And soon we began experiencing it!

But we're nothing special; all believers can experience the power of God in their lives every day. God's power is not just confined to the Bible. It should be the normal Christian experience. Our lives are to be a testimony of how God uses ordinary people to do extraordinary things, and healing is a part of that.

God's will is for all creation to know Him and experience the power of His resurrection (Philippians 3:10). I've witnessed that power. No, I'm no different than you, neither have I been equipped with a "special anointing." But I have come to realize that God's healing, miracle-working power is available now to whoever will believe it. My hope is that through my experiences (and sometimes steep learning curves), you will grow more confident in God's power in *you* to the point that it spills out to transform your life and the lives of those around you.

As Christians, we know that God has the power to heal. Yet many of us know believers who are sick and in desperate need of a miracle. Is God holding out on us? No. He has given us everything we need to see His miracle-working power in our everyday lives (2 Peter 1:3). According to the Great Commission, miracles (what the Bible calls signs and wonders) follow those who believe (Mark 16:17). In the name of Jesus (and because of His work), believers—that's us—can cast out devils, speak in new tongues, heal the sick, and expect divine protection!

And he said unto them, Go ye into all the world, and preach the gospel to every creature. He that believeth and is baptized shall be saved; but he that believeth not shall be damned. **And these signs shall follow them that believe; In my name shall they cast out devils;**

they shall speak with new tongues; They shall take up serpents; and if they drink any deadly thing, it shall not hurt them; they shall lay hands on the sick, and they shall recover. So then after the Lord had spoken unto them, he was received up into heaven, and sat on the right hand of God. And they went forth, and preached everywhere, the Lord working with them, and confirming the word with signs following. Amen.

Mark 16:15-20 KJV (emphasis added)

Right before Jesus was received into heaven, He gave believers these final words of direction. They included both authority and a special charge for their continued role in God's kingdom. It's interesting to me that even those who followed Jesus in person had challenges believing everything they had seen and heard. They needed Jesus to reassure them of their purpose.

Then the eleven disciples went away into Galilee, into a mountain where Jesus had appointed them. And when they saw him, they worshipped him: **but some doubted.** And Jesus came and spake unto them, saying, All power is given unto me in heaven and in earth. **Go ye therefore**, and teach all nations, baptizing them in the name of the Father, and of the Son, and of the Holy Ghost: Teaching them to observe all things whatsoever I have commanded you: and, lo, I am with you alway, even unto the end of the world. Amen.

Matthew 28:16-20 KJV (emphasis added)

If Jesus really is the same yesterday, today, and forever, then we can be confident that He has not changed His mind about us or the plans He has for us (Hebrews 13:8). Laying hands on the sick is the believer's duty until the day Jesus returns and we go to heaven where sickness and disease are nonexistent. God has provided healing for His children and commissioned us to appropriate it in the earth. Although not everyone is called into the five-fold ministry, all believers have been called to be part of a great adventure—being the hands and feet of Jesus and representing Him to the uttermost parts of the earth.

As believers, we can lay hands on the sick and expect to see them recover! But there are a few stipulations. "I knew it," you say, "the catch." Not really a catch, more like necessary qualifications. But don't throw in the towel yet—Jesus made these qualifications freely available to all!

The first qualification is **you must be born again** (John 3:7). In order to receive all the good things God has for you, you must relinquish your life to Him and believe in the One He has sent—Jesus (John 6:29). When you recognize your need for a Savior and accept Jesus' sacrifice on the cross as payment for your sin, you make Him the Lord of your life and are saved. One prerequisite to seeing the healing power of God flow from you to others is first receiving the One who is the Healer. This elementary step is commonly overlooked, but we cannot give what we have not first received.

If you cannot remember asking Jesus to be your Lord or if you are not sure that you will spend eternity in heaven, let's pray! This prayer is a simple one, but when you believe it with all your heart, you can be assured that you belong to Jesus forever (Romans 10:9 and Ephesians 1:17).

Jesus, I believe that You are the Son of God. I believe that You died and rose again so that I can have eternal life. I ask You to be Lord of my life, to live inside my heart, and be my Savior. Thank you, Jesus, for paying the price for my sin, and I receive that payment now as I receive Your forgiveness.

Thank You that I am saved and that You now live in me. Amen

If you just prayed this prayer, welcome to the family!

The second qualification for ministering with God's power is to **be baptized in the Holy Spirit with the evidence of speaking in tongues**. This is a separate experience from being born again, though it often happens at the same time as salvation. The baptism in the Holy Spirit is a spiritual baptism of power. It happens when you recognize the Spirit you received when you were born again and accept His power flowing through you. It is not the same as water baptism.

And being assembled together with them, He commanded them not to depart from Jerusalem, but to wait for the Promise of the Father... "**But you shall receive power when the Holy Spirit has come upon you**; and you shall be witnesses to Me in Jerusalem, and in all Judea and Samaria, and to the end of the earth."

Acts 1:4, 8 (emphasis added)

The Bible says even Jesus did not begin to minister until He was empowered with the Holy Spirit. According to Matthew, He did not perform a single miracle before this time, even though He was God (Matthew 3:16-17). Jesus stressed the importance for all believers to wait to minister until they received the baptism of the Holy Spirit. To me, this suggests that the Holy Spirit is not an optional part of ministry; He is vital!

The Greek word we read for "power" in Acts 1:8 is translated as "strength, ability, and power for performing miracles; an inherent power residing in a thing or person by virtue of its nature; a power that consists of or rests upon armies, forces or hosts; resources arising from numbers; and a moral excellence including the power and influence belonging to riches and wealth" (Strong's Concordance, s.v. "power"). To paraphrase this, power is the supernatural ability and influence of the kingdom of heaven living on the inside of you, putting limitless resources at your disposal, and giving you physical and moral provision, protection, favor, and ability. I could certainly use that kind of power!

Without the baptism in the Holy Spirit, how can we possibly minister effectively? Can we even live our own lives effectively? Without this type of power, even if someone received healing, how would they stay well? Ephesians says it is the supernatural power of God flowing through us that enables us to withstand the wiles of the devil (Ephesians 6:13). One reason we have so many people believing the Bible, sharing the Gospel, and praying for the sick without seeing results is that they don't have the power of the Holy Spirit inside them. It was the Holy Spirit in Jesus that enabled Him to operate in power and destroy the works of the enemy.

> God anointed Jesus of Nazareth with the Holy Spirit and with power, who went about doing good and healing all who were oppressed by the devil, for God was with Him.
>
> Acts 10:38

When Jesus was still with the disciples, He gave them very clear instructions as to their purpose and the authority they were to use in His name. He "called His twelve disciples together and gave them power and authority over all demons, and to cure diseases. He sent them to preach the kingdom of God and to heal the sick" (Luke 9:1-2).

> And these signs will follow those who believe: **In My name** they will cast out demons; they will speak with new tongues; they will take up serpents; and if they drink anything deadly, it will by no means hurt them; they will lay hands on the sick, and they will recover.
>
> Mark 16:17-18 (emphasis added)

Even though these twelve men had Jesus as their personal mentor, they still struggled to grasp the extent of what they were given. On many occasions, this was painfully obvious and caused Jesus great distress.

> On the same day, when evening had come, He said to them, "Let us cross over to the other side." Now when they had left the multitude, they took Him along in the

boat as He was. And other little boats were also with Him. And a great windstorm arose, and the waves beat into the boat, so that it was already filling. But He was in the stern, asleep on a pillow. And they awoke Him and said to Him, "Teacher, do You not care that we are perishing?" Then He arose and rebuked the wind, and said to the sea, "Peace, be still!" And the wind ceased and there was a great calm. But He said to them, "Why are you so fearful? How is it that you have no faith?" And they feared exceedingly, and said to one another, "Who can this be, that even the wind and the sea obey Him!"

Mark 4:35-41

I know we've often read this story, but do you realize that God was in the boat with them? Jesus told the disciples they were using the boat to cross to the other side of the lake. The storm was not unexpected. Jesus knew it was coming, yet He told the disciples to go anyway. They were going to make it! Jesus would not have told them to do something that they could not have achieved.

However, during the storm, the disciples (not yet grounded in faith) went from, "This could be scary," to "God help! We're going to die!" in nearly a breath. They took their eyes off Jesus and focused on their surroundings. The moment Jesus calmed the storm, the disciples were astounded at His authority. They did not fully appreciate who was with them in the boat or the authority He had given them. The disciples didn't need Jesus' help that night. They had everything within themselves to get across that lake; they just didn't realize it.

Like us, unbelief often challenged the disciples. Shortly after their literal mountaintop experience on the Mount of Transfiguration, the disciples were faced with a ministry challenge they couldn't deal with.

> Then one of the crowd answered and said, "Teacher, I brought You my son, who has a mute spirit. And wherever it seizes him, it throws him down; he foams at the mouth, gnashes his teeth, and becomes rigid. So I spoke to Your disciples, that they should cast it out, but they could not." He answered him and said, "O faithless generation, how long shall I be with you? How long shall I bear with you? Bring him to Me."

> Mark 9:17-19

Until the Holy Spirit came, the disciples experienced limited ministry results, despite the fact that Jesus walked with them. The disciples were great examples of how God chooses ordinary people to do extraordinary things! No different from many of us, they grappled with lack of confidence, insecurity, and unbelief. They never did things perfectly, but with the Holy Spirit's help, they accomplished mighty things for the kingdom.

We can see the difference the Holy Spirit made in their lives if we look at them before and after the Day of Pentecost. These ordinary men lived and travelled with Jesus for three years. They ate together, slept together, and shared every thought with each other. You would think that, of all people, they would be the most sure in the faith. But before the Holy Spirit came, they deserted Jesus in His greatest hour of need (Mark 14:50). How could they do that? How could they doubt who Jesus was? The Son of God was in their midst! Yet when they saw Jesus, He was completely man. They saw Him in the morning when He'd just woken up. They saw Him with His hair adrift, with dirt on His face, and smelling like He needed a bath. Even though they walked with Jesus, they still had to learn (like believers do today) who He was and who they were as God's children. It took the Holy Spirit to teach them these things.

On the Day of Pentecost, after those in the upper room were filled with the Holy Spirit, power and boldness came upon the disciples. Instead of hiding away in fear of their lives and mourning the loss of their king, now they were out preaching in the streets! Peter, the one who denied even knowing Jesus, led the first revival meeting, and three thousand people received salvation. Their boldness to witness for Christ was evident to everyone who saw the disciples. Acts says even the religious leaders noticed the difference.

> Now when they saw the boldness of Peter and John, and perceived that they were uneducated and untrained men, they marveled. And they realized that they had been with Jesus. And seeing the man who had been healed standing with them, they could say nothing against it. But when they had commanded them to go aside out of the council, they conferred among themselves, saying, "What shall we do to these men? For, indeed, that a notable miracle has been done through them is evident to all who dwell in Jerusalem, and we cannot deny it."
>
> Acts 4:13-16

The power of God gave the disciples confidence and authority. People began to stop and listen to what they had to say. Even
in the face of persecution and arrest, they refused to be intimi-
dated. The enemy's fear tactics and threats only furthered their
zeal and commitment to the cause of Christ. God was clearly
with them—the evidence stood right next to them! Even their
speech changed following the baptism of the Holy Spirit. Look
at Peter's prayer in Acts chapter four:

> "Now, Lord, look on their threats, and grant to Your ser-
> vants that with all boldness they may speak Your word,
> by stretching out Your hand to heal, and that signs and
> wonders may be done through the name of Your holy
> Servant Jesus." And when they had prayed, the place
> where they were assembled together was shaken; and
> they were all filled with the Holy Spirit, and they spoke
> the word of God with boldness.
>
> Acts 4:29-31

The word "hand" in this verse actually means much more than
a physical appendage. Translated from the original text, it reads
"power, might, or instrument of God" (Strong's Concordance, s.v.
"hand"). Wow! To think that when we stretch out our hands, we
become instruments of the mighty power of God! Because the
Holy Spirit is in us, we can speak the Word of God with boldness
and be strong in faith (Jude 20) just like the disciples were. We can
even see miracles performed through our hands!

"But how do I know the Holy Spirit is for me?" you ask.
Just like the disciples and the rest of the 120 who received the

first outpouring of the Holy Spirit met no special requirements other than believing on Jesus, we as children of God can receive the Spirit's baptism too (Acts 2:39). God wants to give us everything we need to live successful, healthy, prosperous lives. This includes the supernatural power of the Holy Spirit. It is a promise for every believer.

> For everyone who asks receives; the one who seeks finds; and to the one who knocks the door will be opened... If you then, though you are evil, know how to give good gifts to your children, how much more will your Father in heaven give the Holy Spirit to those who ask him!
>
> Luke 11:10, 13

The only thing we have to do is ask, believe, and receive!

Lord, I know that I need Your supernatural power to live my life, and I want to receive everything that You have for me. Please fill me with Your Holy Spirit. I believe, and I receive Him now. Thank You for baptizing me. I thank You Lord that the Holy Spirit now lives in me and that I can speak in tongues.

"Do I have to speak in tongues?" you ask. Let me encourage you. The Holy Spirit has a big job. He reveals the Word to us, inspires our words, operates through us in spiritual gifts, and empowers us to live the Christian life. The gift of speaking in tongues comes as part of that package (Acts 2:4).

Praying in tongues is an outward proof of the baptism of the Holy Spirit. It is a huge benefit to believers for a number of reasons. First, when we pray in tongues, our spirit prays. This can be very useful during moments of doubt, when we don't know how we should pray, or if we are feeling fearful or struggling to focus our minds on God rather than circumstances. Secondly, while praying in tongues, the Holy Spirit reveals to us "hidden mysteries" (Job 12:22). He gives us wisdom and revelation. This is especially useful when praying for healing for a person who does not know the problem or if you are ministering to someone who speaks another language and there is no one to interpret. The Holy Spirit knows all things and language is no barrier to Him. Praying in tongues also builds up our faith (Jude 20). It takes faith to pray in tongues! Praying in tongues makes no human sense, and our brains often try to convince us that it is make-believe, but it is a language between us and God.

"Can I pray for others without speaking in tongues?" Absolutely. I was born again for twelve years before I was able to pray in tongues, and I prayed for lots of people in that time. (At the time, I did not understand that tongues was available. And when I did finally encounter it, the fear of the unfamiliar kept me from receiving it.) However, I have found the gift of tongues so valuable when ministering that I rarely pray now without a combination of English and tongues. Praying for a few seconds in the Spirit as I lay hands on someone often gives me the direction and insight I need to minister to the heart of their problem. Tongues helps me focus my mind on the Lord and tunes my hearing to His voice so I can be more effective.

One time, an elderly lady came to me for prayer, explaining that she was suffering from numerous symptoms she didn't want to disclose. She was very thin and weak and obviously discouraged. As she closed her eyes in expectation, I felt a deep love for this vulnerable stranger. My heart ached for this lady I had known for only minutes. Although she never mentioned it, I was aware that she wondered if God cared about her. So many people had prayed for her without any effect that she was ready to give up on God: "Hope deferred makes the heart sick" (Proverbs 13:12). As I prayed in tongues, I heard, "Speak to her liver." So I commanded her liver to function normally in Jesus' name. She began to weep. Finally, a small smile crept across her face. Not only had her symptoms left, but she knew that only God could have told me how to pray for her. This lady needed more than physical healing. She needed to experience the love of God. She needed to know that He loved her so much He would speak to her through a complete stranger. The Holy Spirit working through me was the confirmation she had been searching for.

All miracles must start in the heart. No matter where we are in our walk with God, we must understand it's not about us; it's about Jesus. We are all growing in our revelation of God; we are all learning. So while on the inside we may feel totally out of our depth, Jesus in us is everything we need to be effective ministers of God's life (Romans 8:11). The more we step out, the more we will experience God working through us, and the bolder we will become to believe God.

And we have such trust through Christ toward God. Not that we are sufficient of ourselves to think of anything as being from ourselves, but our sufficiency is from God, who also made us sufficient as ministers of the new covenant, not of the letter but of the Spirit; for the letter kills, but the Spirit gives life.

2 Corinthians 3:4-6

That the sharing of your faith may become effective by the acknowledgment of every good thing which is in you in Christ Jesus.

Philemon 6

two

FLIPPING THE SWITCH

The will of God is one of the most disputed areas of doctrine in the church today. For many years, I was satisfied with the standard response I received from elders in the faith that "you never can know the will or mind of God. His ways are higher than our ways." This explanation was churned out following every episode of tragedy, confusion, hardship, sickness, or roadblock. It seemed God received credit for as much evil as He did good. I loved God with all my heart but could not understand how, if He was so loving, it could be His plan for us to suffer in so many ways.

Even though I had dealt with sickness my entire life, when my daughter got sick, the elders' standard statement no longer satisfied me. Every time I read the New Testament, I saw that it was full of examples of miracles and healings. I searched the Bible for an expiration date to these manifestations but found none. My simple logic told me that if this same power was indeed at work in me now like it was in Jesus, then I should be seeing miracles and healings like Jesus did (Romans 8:11). Perhaps all I'd been taught was wrong. Perhaps my thinking was wrong. It comforted me to know that if something was wrong on my end in my thinking, I could change me!

About 18 months before my daughter became really sick, I received an invitation to attend a midday women's Bible study. This small group of ladies belonged to a different church than me, but I was drawn to them. As young mothers with a passion for God, this group of ladies wasn't afraid to show their zeal. They believed in speaking in tongues, but I noticed they did not exude a fake spirituality. They spoke like the people in the Bible. They talked to God like a friend. And the most intriguing thing for me was that God talked back! These ladies had something I did not, and I wanted it! They soon became my close friends and demonstrated Jesus to me in a way I had never experienced. The Holy Spirit was a strange and mysterious concept to me, yet this group provided a safe place in which the gifts of the Spirit could operate. It was here that I first heard God speak to me.

When I first heard God speak, I feared I may have experienced some mental derangement—probably from a lack of sleep. (After all, any mother caring for three children under the age of three, who changes a minimum of 20 diapers a day, could expect a few damaged brain cells, right?) Then I got an epiphany; God always spoke—He was always there—but now I was finally listening (Isaiah 51:16, Hebrews 13:5, and Matthew 13:15).

I sat at our next Bible study gathering in as near a silence as one possibly could with a herd of toddlers dissembling the room next door and practiced listening to whatever the Lord had to say. I was certain that the only reason God would ever speak to me was to bring correction, so I was always careful to make sure every sin was promptly confessed. I even included a blanket statement at the end of my prayers: "And please forgive me for anything else I forgot to mention. Amen." Because of my diligence to confess my sins, I was confident the Lord had nothing else to say to me. Still, I sat as requested, cleared my mind of wandering thoughts, and listened. To my surprise, thoughts began to pop into my head, which seemed to come from nowhere. With one eye tightly shut and the other slightly open, I shot a glance around the room to see if anyone was the source of the conversation going on in my head. It was then I realized the Lord was putting thoughts in my mind!

As I mentioned before, I had dealt with sickness forever. It was a source of strain in my daily life and also in my spiritual life. I was reading my Bible and just couldn't reconcile the differences I was seeing between the early church and the church I attended. I couldn't understand how God could be described as loving and yet be responsible for much of the suffering and heartache ascribed to Him. I tried to recall all the people I had seen prayed for and healed. I had actually never seen or heard of anyone receiving healing in a spiritual way. I knew of people who thanked God for healing them, and I am sure that He had a part to play in it, but they all followed some course of medical treatment. Rather than seeing this as a matter of divine intervention, the nurse part of me concluded that medicine had done its job. In my experience, Christians prayed for the sick more from duty than with any real expectancy. We always ended our prayers with, "If it be Thy will, Lord," and that hardly seemed a guarantee. But how could we know if God was in a good mood? Or if the person being prayed for deserved healing? Or even if God still healed? Then I recalled reading in James:

> Is anyone among you sick? Let him call for the elders of the church, and let them pray over him, anointing him with oil in the name of the Lord. And the prayer of faith will save the sick, and the Lord will raise him up. And if he has committed sins, he will be forgiven.

> James 5:14-15

I noticed it wasn't just any prayer that saved the sick. Healing required a prayer of faith. I thought, *Well, if faith is to be sure of the things I hope for and certain of the things I cannot see* (Hebrews 11:1), *then praying with faith involves a level of certainty, not wonder.* Apparently, when James wrote about praying for the sick, he was not asking God to heal them but expecting to see them healed. No wonder I hadn't seen or heard of any healings! There was clearly no shortage of sick or praying people, but there was a shortage of faith. That day I realized that faith has to be present for healing to be received. As I sat there processing these thoughts and listening, I heard something that sounded so alien to me I knew it could never have come from my flesh. I heard:

> *Carlie, you have held Me outside of the epilepsy. You don't need to. I want to take it from you, if you want me to. In two weeks' time, you can be free from this if you choose to be. Flip the switch.*

In my mind, I saw a light switch. I knew that if I flipped the switch, the epilepsy I had struggled with since childhood would be gone.

The profoundness of this statement hit me like a freight train. If I had been talking, I would have become speechless. Seconds before God spoke, I was a sufferer, a victim of life and circumstance just trying to survive. Now I understood that the God of the universe had put the power to "choose life" in my hands. A hundred questions raced through my head. Could it really be that simple? Do I really have a choice to change my circumstances? Can my thoughts and beliefs really change my physical condition?

According to Scripture, we do have a choice to make. Life is not automatic. We have to choose God's blessing over the devil's curse.

> I call heaven and earth as witnesses today against you, that **I have set before you life and death**, blessing and cursing; therefore **choose life**, that both you and your descendants may live.
>
> Deuteronomy 30:19 (emphasis added)

Life is meant to be a blessing, but receiving that blessing starts with a choice—our choice.

God put the choice to live before me. Looking around at the other ladies in the study group, I could see others opening their eyes, and I knew it was time to go. Fearing I had lost my mind and that others could see it, I said nothing. I knew I would have a lot to think about during the next two weeks.

I continued to keep the afternoon's events to myself. I didn't even share what had happened with my husband. I was certain the account would sound as ridiculous to him as it did to me. I decided that if what I'd experienced really was God speaking and not some strange side effect from one of the dozen or so medications I ingested daily, then I wanted Him to show me it was real. My brain tried very hard to convince me that I had just imagined the whole incident, but I knew it was of God. Every time I searched my heart, I found that the thought of being healed filled me with dread.

I know it sounds silly, but I was afraid of being healed. All my life, I had been sick in some way. I hated to admit it, but a part of me needed to be sick. It had become a way of life, a part of my identity, an excuse when I needed something to hide behind. It made me special. I was ashamed and embarrassed at my own neediness, but I didn't know how to be well. However, I knew my flesh hadn't dreamt up the notion of being healed.

I barely noticed as two weeks ticked by. I was too busy think- ing about all the ways I had adapted my daily life around the disease of epilepsy. I began to notice the small details of my life: the drug routine, the hospital appointments and admissions, the babysitter who came to sit for me because I could not be left alone with my children. I noticed the locks we installed at the top of each door so I could contain the toddlers in a safe place when I felt a seizure coming on. I remembered the number of times I had awoken in a strange hospital room wondering who I was and where the twigs in my hair had come from. I remem- bered meeting my baby girl for the first time and thinking, *How do I know that she is mine?* (I was mid-seizure during her delivery and unconscious.)

I came to realize that not being able to work or drive or function independently as a healthy adult had messed with my thinking. Epilepsy had begun to identify me, slowly taking over larger and larger pieces of my life. It dictated how I spent my time, where and with whom I could associate. It told me how to plan my day, what to eat and when to sleep. It separated me from my family and strained my relationships. Epilepsy had caused financial hardships and dictated my future. But worse than all of these things, it was sucking away my confidence and self-worth like a disgusting parasite.

And yet, the thought of being normal and healthy terrified me. I had no track record of health. It was foreign ground to me. Epilepsy had given me a crutch, a way out when I didn't want to do something. If I was normal, I could work a job and drive a car. I would have nothing left to make me special. That was the bottom of the barrel, an ugly truth in my heart that I didn't even know was there. Epilepsy made me feel special.

Once all these dirty little secrets surfaced within me, I just could not squeeze them all back into the jar they came from. Now that I knew they were there, I couldn't "unknow" them, and I didn't really want to. My heart was changing. Ever so gently, the Holy Spirit was convicting me of the dark insecurities of my heart so He could show me my salvation.

> The thief does not come except to steal, and to kill, and
> to destroy. I have come that they may have life, and that
> they may have it more abundantly.
>
> John 10:10

This verse revolutionized my thought life. For the first time with the Holy Spirit's help, I saw that the enemy came to kill, steal, and destroy me physically, emotionally, and spiritually. But Jesus came to give me life and show me how to live it. Even though it was uncomfortable for a while, the Holy Spirit guided me into truth so He could bring healing, peace, love, joy, and freedom to my life (John 16:13). I began to consider what life would be like without epilepsy. I thought of what it would be like to plan and follow my dreams, to have enough energy for the day, to walk down the stairs and know that I would make it to the bottom without having a seizure. I dreamed of what life would look like if I no longer fell asleep without warning or rocked myself into a fetal position when the side effects of my disease cramped my muscles. I thought of how it would be to walk alone, to drive, to explore, to not have to explain this condition or take medication or stay in the hospital or even go to the doctor anymore. My dream was huge!

But even bigger than my dream of life without epilepsy was the miracle that no one ever saw. The biggest part of my healing was the revelation that I was special simply because I had become a child of God. I didn't need to be afraid; God was with me. He would always be my hiding place.

He who dwells in the secret place of the Most High shall abide under the shadow of the Almighty. I will say of the LORD, "He is my refuge and my fortress; my God, in Him I will trust." Surely He shall deliver you from the snare of the fowler and from the perilous pestilence... "With long life I will satisfy him, and show him My salvation."

Psalm 91:1-3, 16

This passage showed me that if put my trust in the Lord, He would deliver me from epilepsy. I was finally ready to give the disease that had taken over my life to the Lord. I knew I was no longer powerless in this situation. I knew it was my decision to accept or reject the gift God had for me, and I knew my decision would determine whether or not I continued to allow the enemy to steal from my life. I was ready to flip the switch. I knew that the moment I flipped the switch in my mind, epilepsy would be gone.

Being rather preoccupied, I had forgotten that two weeks was the timeframe God gave me in prayer. On the way to my women's Bible study that Friday, I wondered if everything that I had heard, felt, and experienced of God had really happened. I had never heard of anyone talking with God like I had. I'd never heard of anyone being healed or seen anyone be healed. What if I was crazy? This was probably heresy; I was going to die, struck by lightening for stupidity or blasphemy. *Well at least I haven't spoken out my thoughts or told anyone… But what if it really was God?* I decided to test the matter. If it really had been God speaking to me, then someone would offer to pray for me at Bible study. If no one offered to pray for me, then I would chalk the whole thing up to my imagination and forgot about it all.

The ladies gathered as usual with the little kids playing in the hallway, quietly dismantling the house. Occasionally the conversation broke to allow a mom to apply an ice pack to newly slapped skin or attend to a pungent bottom, but nothing out of the ordinary happened, and suddenly, it was time to go. Rounding up my tribe and heading for the front door, one of the ladies stopped and turned towards me. "I need to pray for you," she said.

I don't remember what she prayed. I know it was quick, a micro prayer, which didn't add an "if it be Thy will" to its end. Immediately I felt heat throughout my body, and in my mind, I flipped the switch of epilepsy off. Nothing on the outside of me changed, but I knew it was done. I couldn't wait to get back and tell my husband what had happened!

He was not as thrilled as I had hoped he would be. He hadn't had two weeks of preparation like I had, nor had God told him the things that He had spoken to me. In my husband's mind, he was still the one holding my hand every time I was checked into the ICU, teetering between life and death. He looked at me, saw nothing different, looked at our three little ones, and said, "You're going to die and leave me with three children to raise, aren't you?"

He was even less happy when I told him that I wouldn't be needing my medications anymore. When I mentioned I had stopped taking them, he about flipped his own switch! In the past, if I was even a half hour late taking the medications, I would have a seizure. My husband tried his best to convince me to take them, and honestly, I don't blame him. If I were in his position, I would have done the same. We had zero experiences with God's healing and a long history of medical intervention.

I really wanted to reassure him, but I knew that I could not take that medication. My healing was so real to me that however much I respected my husband, I could not go against that which I knew was of God. I had absolute peace in that decision, and to this day, it is the only time I have purposely defied my husband. (Disclaimer: God's Word trumps human words every time, but you had better know that it is God!) Since then, my life has gone from having multiple seizures a day to having zero! I stopped all medications without experiencing any side effects. This, in itself, was supernatural. In the past, each time I had my medication levels adjusted, it sent my body into a tailspin that often landed me in the hospital. Even though I couldn't say with 100 percent certainty at the time that I would never have another seizure (I had no evidence to prove I was healed), I was absolutely convinced that it was God's will for me to be healed. And I have been walking in it for over ten years!

The Bible says we receive from God by grace through faith (Ephesians 2:8). Faith simply believes God above everything else, and it works by love (Galatians 5:6). When we know how much God loves us, we know His will and faith is born where the will of God is known. If I hadn't known it was God's will to heal me, I could never have put faith in His promise of healing. When I returned home the day I was healed, I asked the Lord, "Why now?" I had been sick for such a long time. Why had He not spoken to me before? God spoke a scripture to me that answered my questions. He said:

> And in Lystra a certain man without strength in his feet was sitting, a cripple from his mother's womb, who had never walked. This man heard Paul speaking. Paul, observing him intently and **seeing that he had faith to be healed,** said with a loud voice, "Stand up straight on your feet!" And he leaped and walked.
>
> Acts 14:8-10

When I read this, I knew that I was healed because for the first time, I had been in a position to believe God for healing. My faith was active. Before I heard the truth regarding God's will to heal, I couldn't believe. You see, faith is the vehicle by which we access the promises of God.

In Acts 14, the crippled man Paul prayed for had never walked. You can bet that crippling condition he experienced had become a part of his identity. Yet the day Paul observed him, something changed. The man heard Paul speak, and he believed. The Word tells us, "Faith comes by hearing and hearing by the Word of God" (Romans 10:17). It also says:

> For the hearts of this people have grown dull. Their ears are hard of hearing, And their eyes they have closed, Lest they should see with their eyes and hear with their ears, Lest they should understand with their hearts and turn, So that I should heal them.
>
> Matthew 13:15

We need to hear the truth regarding healing, and we need to listen. God had to speak healing to me because there was no one else around to do it, but before I could hear His voice, I had to put myself in a quiet spot to actively listen. Once we hear, we have to believe and act upon the truth we've heard. I'm sure God tried to reach out to me before, but healing is first understood at a heart level. His will for me hadn't changed that morning; it was always for me to be well. God wants all His children to be healed.

And it happened when He was in a certain city, that behold, a man who was full of leprosy saw Jesus; and he fell on his face and implored Him, saying, "Lord, if You are willing, You can make me clean." Then He put out His hand and touched him, saying, **"I am willing**; be cleansed."

Luke 5:12-13 (emphasis added)

In the Gospels, we see that every person who approached Jesus for healing was fully restored. Jesus was always willing to help them. If God's will was for us to be sick, Jesus wouldn't have gone about "doing good and healing all who were oppressed by the devil" (Acts 10:38). If healing wasn't always God's will, He wouldn't have provided it with salvation, deliverance, and prosperity as part of the atonement.

Beloved, I wish above all things that thou mayest prosper and be in health, even as thy soul prospereth.

3 John 1:2 KJV

Even in the Old Testament, God's will was to heal (Exodus 15:26). Seeing that He is a God that "changes not," we can be assured that He has not had a change of heart on the matter! (Malachi 3:6).

Bless the Lord, O my soul; And all that is within me, bless His holy name! Bless the Lord, O my soul, And forget not all His benefits: **Who forgives all your iniquities, Who heals all your diseases.**

Psalm 103:1-3 (emphasis added)

three

WHAT YOU DON'T KNOW CAN HURT YOU

Many people believe that God can heal. They believe He has the power to heal, but they often don't know if He will do it for them. After I was healed of epilepsy, my daughter was diagnosed with a deadly auto-immune disease. Even though I saw God heal me, I still did not have a complete understanding of His will regarding healing. I knew God wanted to heal me, but I didn't know if that was just a one-time event. Although my husband and I prayed for Hannah to be healed, we were not able to pray a prayer of faith because we did not know if it was God's will for her to be healed. The truth is, healing is not a matter of God deciding who gets healed and who doesn't. His mind about us was made up long before we were born!

The payment for our healing was made at the cross (1 Peter 2:24). God provided healing for us at the same time He settled our sin. In Jesus' time, most people did not doubt that He could heal—they saw it happening all the time—but they did doubt that He could forgive sin. This is interesting to me because in the culture of Jesus' day, God could only relate to mankind through physical signs. The Holy Spirit had not yet come to dwell in people's hearts; He came upon individuals for a particular purpose and left. The people of Jesus' time would have known the mighty miracles performed by the prophets (parting of the Red Sea, water from the rock, fire from heaven, healing of Naaman) by heart.

Once the word got out that Jesus was doing miracles, crowds flocked to Him because they knew what the power of God looked like. They would have thought, *It's the Messiah* or at the very least, *A prophet!* When the paralytic man's friends lowered him through the roof to Jesus, the Pharisees never questioned Jesus' power to heal him. The challenge for the religious crowd was in Jesus' ability to forgive sin. That is why Jesus asked them, "What is easier to say, arise take up your bed and walk or your sins have been forgiven" (Mark 2:9). These people had never seen sins forgiven without a sacrifice. For them to understand that Jesus would become that sacrifice was difficult!

Today, people struggle with the opposite. They accept their forgiveness of sin but doubt the possibility of physical healing. I suspect that this is because people find it easier to relate to a God they cannot see. Now that the Holy Spirit resides within us, God speaks to us Spirit to spirit. He does not need to rely on outward signs to communicate with us. Much of our relationship with God is unseen. So many Christians internalize their relationships with God and allow little outward evidence of their faith to show. Healing is a challenging outward expression of the power of God that some would rather ignore. However, there are many verses of scripture that pair healing and forgiveness of sin together.

> Confess your trespasses to one another, and pray for one another, that you may be healed. The effective, fervent prayer of a righteous man avails much.
>
> James 5:16

> Who forgives all your sins and heals all your diseases.
>
> Psalm 103:3 NIV

> For whosoever shall call upon the name of the Lord shall be saved.
>
> Romans 10:13 KJV

The word used here for "saved" is *sozo*. In the original Greek text, one word often had several meanings. Unfortunately, these were lost when the Bible was translated into English. In Greek, *sozo* means, "to save a suffering one (from perishing)," including suffering from disease. It also means "to make well, heal, restore to health, to save, to keep safe and sound, to rescue or deliver from danger, destruction, or peril" (Strong's Concordance, s.v. "saved"). So Romans 10:13 could be written as, "Whoever calls on the name of the Lord shall be healed, forgiven, and delivered from destruction."

With all the scriptural evidence, why would someone not believe in healing? There are many reasons why people struggle to believe that healing still happens today. Most people who believe in God accept that He has the power to heal; they simply have never experienced healing. I fell into this category. My low expectations were constantly confirmed by my circumstances, thus reinforcing the notion that God either doesn't heal anymore or that healing is mysteriously tied to God's good mood (and He apparently is never in a good mood). This understanding could be called lack of knowledge, and it results primarily from little or wrong teaching.

There are also those who believe that healing (and the other gifts of the Spirit) passed away with the last apostles. Since we already know that it takes faith to receive the things of God, naturally their lack of faith hinders the gifts from operating in their lives. Unfortunately, the lack of evidence around them only compounds their belief that the gifts have ceased. James says they "have not because they ask not" (James 4:2).

Some of my friends were raised in this belief. They had never seen any manifestations of healing, prophesy, or tongues, and their experience only served to reinforce their beliefs. Then one day their child became very sick and was not expected to live. The doctors offered them no hope and neither did their church. Yet as loving parents, they were desperate to see their child healed, and this was the incentive they needed to open their hearts to the truth. Laying aside their preconceived ideas about God, they began to search for the truth about Him in the Bible. They discovered Isaiah 53, which says:

> Who has believed our report? And to whom has the arm of the Lord been revealed? For He shall grow up before Him as a tender plant, and as a root out of dry ground. He has no form or comeliness; and when we see

Him, there is no beauty that we should desire Him. He
is despised and rejected by men, a Man of sorrows and
acquainted with grief. And we hid, as it were, our faces
from Him; He was despised, and we did not esteem Him.
Surely He has borne our griefs and carried our sorrows;
yet we esteemed Him stricken, smitten by God, and af-
flicted. But He was wounded for our transgressions, He
was bruised for our iniquities; the chastisement for our
peace was upon Him, and by His stripes we are healed.

Isaiah 53:1-5

This book prophesies the birth, death, and resurrection of
Jesus. It describes how Jesus would be revealed as God's Son and
what His death would accomplish for those who believe. If we
break apart verse four using the original language, we'll find that
it actually reads, "Certainly Jesus is prepared to accept and carry
away from us our sickness, disease, and pain" (Strong's Concordance, s.v. "borne"). Even verse five speaks of how Jesus' death
would provide for our physical healing and wholeness! We see
the fulfillment of this prophesy as it is repeated in 1 Peter.

Who Himself bore our sins in His own body on the tree,
that we, having died to sins, might live for righteousness—by whose stripes you were healed.

1 Peter 2:24

The only difference is that this time, the writer used the word
"healed"—the past tense form. Why? Because Jesus had already
accomplished healing for us! He finished the work on His cross.

45

We are healed, cured, and made whole by the blood of Christ. God has completely restored us and forgiven our sin. Amen!

Satan works hard to hide this truth from believers. When he can no longer hide it, he twists it so when people who know God is good experience sickness, they believe God must have hidden some blessing in it. But Deuteronomy 28 clearly lists sickness and disease as a curse (Deuteronomy 28:15, 21-22, 27-28, 35, 59-61). The good news is that Jesus redeemed us from this curse; it no longer has a hold over believers.

> Christ has redeemed us from the curse of the law, having become a curse for us (for it is written, "Cursed is everyone who hangs on a tree").
>
> Galatians 3:13

Yet, there are many who choose not to receive what is rightfully theirs. They continue to live defeated lives, responding to sickness the same way the world does. They measure God's promises by their experiences. It is easier for them to explain the lack of supernatural activity in their lives as God withholding something or teaching them something than it is to accept their responsibility to believe. But Psalm 84 says:

> For the Lord God is a sun and shield: the Lord will give grace and glory: **no good thing will he withhold** from those who walk uprightly.
>
> Psalm 84:11 (emphasis added)

The idea that God is withholding good from His children makes no sense scripturally. Jesus never put sickness on anyone.

He never refused to heal. This idea doesn't even make natural sense. My parents were unsaved until my late teens. No one in my family knew Christ. Yet even as heathens, we knew a good gift from a bad one! Parents naturally give everything they have to save the life of their child; they certainly do not withhold a cure if it is in their power to give it. But believers get this all mixed up because they have a wrong understanding of the true nature of God. God is good. Satan is bad. It's simple, yet many have this confused. They have been deceived into thinking that sickness can be good and that God can use sickness to teach His children valuable lessons they can't learn otherwise. They believe that God allows bad things to happen to them for their overall good.

This is not true! It's a perfect example of what the scriptures describe as "calling good, evil and evil good" (Isaiah 5:20). Satan thrives on this belief because as long as God is getting the credit for his evil, he can run roughshod over our lives undetected. Not only do Christians die and suffer, but they live in defeat thinking it is helping them testify of God. Not only is their testimony hindered, but their own relationship with God is affected. It is impossible to pray a prayer of faith or enter into an intimate relationship with a God when you believe He may subject you to some disaster for your own good. Hebrews tells us we can come before God's throne with boldness! He is our loving Father from whom comes every good and perfect gift! We shouldn't be afraid of Him. We should celebrate our relationship with Him and expect Him to be whom He has portrayed Himself to be— not whom others have accused Him of being.

Having therefore, brethren, boldness to enter into the holiest by the blood of Jesus, by a new and living way, which he hath consecrated for us, through the veil, that is to say, his flesh; and [having] an high priest over the house of God; let us draw near with a true heart in full assurance of faith, having our hearts sprinkled from an evil conscience, and our bodies washed with pure water.

Hebrews 10:19-22 KJV

Every good gift and every perfect gift is from above, and cometh down from the Father of lights, with whom is no variableness, neither shadow of turning.

James 1:17 KJV

Faith is how we get what is in our spirit (what God has given us) to manifest in our bodies. Faith puts our trust and confidence in the finished work of the cross. The provision for our healing was in the sacrifice of Jesus Christ 2000 years ago, we don't need to wait on God to heal us—He already did everything necessary to ensure we can walk in health and healing. We simply receive healing by faith, the same way we receive salvation. Just like it's impossible to be a "little bit saved," it's impossible for God to break apart the package deal of what Christ provided on the cross.

Healing has been provided, but we must respond to it in faith in order to receive that provision. Jesus taught His disciples to speak to their mountains and take authority over them in His name. Today, many people do not understand that His authority is still ours; it was given to us the moment Jesus came to live in us. Now we have the power and authority to overcome sickness and disease with our words. When Jesus said speak to your mountain, He meant it!

> So Jesus answered and said to them, "Have faith in God. For assuredly, I say to you, whoever says to this mountain, 'Be removed and be cast into the sea,' and does not doubt in his heart, but believes that those things he says will be done, he will have whatever he says. Therefore I say to you, whatever things you ask when you pray, believe that you receive them, and you will have them."
>
> Mark 11:22-24

The misunderstanding of authority often shows up in the way we pray. Many people beg and plead with God to do for them what He told them to do for themselves. They wonder why they never see the promises of God manifest in their lives. But God has already worked on our behalf in the person of Jesus. Asking God to heal us when He already did, leads to confusion and disappointment in the Church. Instead, we should follow Jesus' example of prayer—I'm sure He knew what He was doing!

> But Jesus rebuked him, saying, "Be quiet, and come out of him!"
>
> Mark 1:25

> So He stood over her and rebuked the fever, and it left her. And immediately she arose and served them.
>
> Luke 4:39

But He put them all outside, took her by the hand and called, saying, "Little girl, arise."

Luke 8:54

And He said to her, "Daughter, your faith has made you well. Go in peace, and be healed of your affliction."

Mark 5:34

"I say to you, arise, take up your bed, and go to your house."

Mark 2:11

In these few examples, we see that Jesus' prayers were always effective and surprisingly concise. Jesus did not ask God to come down and fix the problems He was confronted with. He did not pray "if it be Thy will," because He knew it was His will. This understanding enabled Jesus to speak directly to each issue with authority. He put that same authority into our hands at the cross, and according to Scripture, that decision has not changed (Malachi 3:6 and Hebrews 13:8).

When God created mankind, He gave them the right to rule and reign over the earth.

Then God blessed them, and God said to them, "Be fruitful and multiply; fill the earth and subdue it; have dominion over the fish of the sea, over the birds of the air, and over every living thing that moves on the earth."

Genesis 1:28

The heaven, even the heavens, are the Lord's; but the
earth He has given to the children of men.

Psalms 115:16

However at the fall, man passed his God-given authority
over to Satan. The death and resurrection of Jesus reversed this
statute as God Almighty took up residence inside His children
through the person of the Holy Spirit. Once and for all, authority was given back to mankind. As children of God, we have
an awesome responsibility to use the authority He's given us to
take authority over the works of the enemy with supernatural,
miracle-working power!

And when He had called His twelve disciples to Him,
He gave them power over unclean spirits, to cast them
out, and to heal all kinds of sickness and all kinds of disease… "Heal the sick, cleanse the lepers, raise the dead,
cast out demons. Freely you have received, freely give."

Matthew 10:1, 8

And He said to them, "I saw Satan fall like lightning
from heaven. Behold, I give you the authority to trample on serpents and scorpions, and over all the power of
the enemy, and nothing shall by any means hurt you."

Luke 10:18-19

Then He called His twelve disciples together and gave
them power and authority over all demons, and to cure
diseases. He sent them to preach the kingdom of God
and to heal the sick.

Luke 9:1-2

If a person does not understand their authority in Christ, they will not exercise it. Sickness is a symptom of Satan trying to trespass in our lives. Because of the blood of Christ, he has no right to do that unless we give it to him. James 4:7 (NIV) says, "Submit yourselves, then, to God. Resist the devil, and he will flee from you." This is an interesting verse. Many Christians willingly submit themselves to God, but they struggle with the middle of the verse, still expecting Satan to flee! Look at it like a simple equation:

Submit to God + Resist the devil = Devil will flee

Resist is not the same as ignore or plead. Resist is a verb. *Strong's Exhaustive Concordance* says that "resist" means "to set one's self against, to withstand, resist, or oppose" (s.v. "resist"). Paul used this same word to describe what we do with the whole armor of God.

> Wherefore take unto you the whole armour of God, that ye may be able to withstand in the evil day, and having done all, to stand.

> Ephesians 6:13 KJV

When we resist the devil, he has no choice but to flee because victory is every believer's guarantee.

> No weapon that is formed against thee shall prosper; and every tongue that shall rise against thee in judgment thou shalt condemn.

> Isaiah 54:17 KJV

You are of God, little children, and have overcome
them, because He who is in you is greater than he who
is in the world!

1 John 4:4

Satan is a defeated enemy. His tactics are merely weapons
formed against us. They cannot prosper once we recognize this
powerful truth and learn to resist him.

Giving thanks unto the Father, which hath made us
meet to be partakers of the inheritance of the saints in
light: Who hath delivered us from the power of dark-
ness, and hath translated us into the kingdom of his
dear Son: In whom we have redemption through his
blood, even the forgiveness of sins.

Colossians 1:12-14 KJV

The devil roams around as a roaring lion seeking whom he
may devour, but he is just an imitator—a fraud (1 Peter 5:8-9).
It is time to stand up, know what belongs to us as believers, and
start living the life Christ died to give us. Refuse to be devoured.
Take yourself off of his menu! The victory is ours, but what we
don't know can hurt us! We are not weak, feeble believers who
must endure life like everyone else. We not only have the hope
of heaven, we have the power of the entire kingdom living inside
us. That is more than enough power to raise the dead, heal the
sick, cast out demons, pay the rent, and overcome depression!

four

MIRACLE GIRL

Hannah is our baby girl, the youngest of our tribe. She was our surprise baby. Having just returned to work, I thought the tiredness I was experiencing was a result of juggling a new job that kept me on my feet all day and being a mom to two small boys. My husband and I talked about waiting several years before having another couple of children, so finding out we were expecting again so soon was overwhelming. I already had two in a stroller; I didn't know where I was going to put another! Ashley, my husband, consoled me with the promise of a dishwasher to ease the strain of busy days, and we began making plans for another little one to join the Terradez tribe!

At this time in my life, I was still struggling with epilepsy. My already difficult pregnancy was made even more so because morning sickness caused me to lose not only most of my meals to the toilet but also the anticonvulsants that I took to control my seizures. As the pregnancy progressed and my hormones desta-bilized the drug levels in my body, the seizures I experienced on

55

a regular basis became uncontrollable. I spent most of my first trimester in the hospital being pumped full of powerful drugs to keep me alive while Hannah was forming in my belly.

My doctors decided that we should make a trip to King's College Hospital in London and meet with the country's top specialists. After various scans and tests, the news at thirty-weeks' gestation was mixed. We discovered we were expecting a baby girl. That was exciting! But we also found that her cerebellum (a large part of the brain responsible for motor control) was missing and that her limbs were deformed. The drugs I was taking for epilepsy caused both of her hands to be bent sideways and all of her digits were deformed. The doctors took us into a side room and asked how we would like to proceed with this pregnancy. It shocked me that suddenly my baby girl had become a pregnancy rather than a person to them.

"I'm going to have my baby!" I responded.

On our way home, we didn't speak about the subject again and continued planning to have a healthy child just like our others. Somewhere in the back of my mind, I had it settled that God had plenty of time to heal Hannah before she was due. I decided it wasn't worth worrying about something I could not change.

Shortly after, Hannah stopped growing in my womb, and I began experiencing three or four seizures each day. My body was tired, and every cell felt like it was screaming, "Deliver this baby!" After 31 hours of labor on January 16, 2003, at 4:25 p.m., Hannah Megan entered the world. She was a perfectly formed, pink, wriggly little girl! God healed Hannah of the deformities seen on her ultrasound and made her brain perfectly complete!

But in the hours following Hannah's arrival, it became clear that she could not control her body temperature.

Although she was born early and was very tiny, the doctors told us that we could take her home. However, less than 24 hours later, we were readmitted. We could tell something was very wrong. Hannah would not wake up. The hospital ran a batch of tests, and since she was jaundiced, lethargic, and not eating, they inserted a feeding tube. A week and a battery of antibiotics later, we were released to go home, but something still felt wrong to me. As a third-time mom, I knew there was a problem with my baby that the doctors had missed.

As the weeks went by, Hannah failed to thrive. She would vomit her ounce of formula every time we fed her. We had to set an alarm through the night to wake her up every two hours to eat because she was so small. Even then, the process of feeding was so slow that she would fall asleep, and we would have to start over. Her vomiting became so regular that any time she coughed, her brothers would run away shouting, "Sick on me. Sick on me!" (They had been on the receiving end of their sister's vomit enough times to know to move.)

Because she struggled so much with milk, we decided to delay introducing solid foods. At nine months old, we finally began experimenting with different purees. It was then we realized her difficulty was swallowing. She would choke and turn blue on every food she tried to swallow. It became so normal to us that we stopped strapping her in the high chair so we could quickly pull her out and flip her upside down to dislodge any food when she began choking. Despite numerous doctor visits and tests, no diagnosis was made, and we watched helplessly as our baby girl struggled in pain.

We were tired. Tired of waking up every hour through the night with a child screaming in pain, tired of washing sheets covered in vomit, tired of being bounced between hospitals and labeled as neurotic parents. Finally, we were referred to a specialist in London. More tests and a surgery gave us a name for Hannah's condition.

After three months of waiting on test results, I had high hopes these doctors—the best in the country—would be able to finally give us some answers, but the appointment didn't go as well as I'd hoped. Walking into the doctor's office piled high with patient notes, peeling wall charts, and the smell of disinfectant, the doctor said, "We have a diagnosis, but we can write what we know about it on the back of a postage stamp. It's possible she'll grow out of it; we just don't know." With that, the doctor scribbled the name of the disease on a yellow sticky note and told us to Google it: eosinophilic enteropathy.

Sticky note in hand, we left with our two-year-old daughter, no more certain of her prognosis than before. At home, we learned everything we could about the condition from doctors around the world. Soon our doctors began asking us for recommendations on Hannah's treatment. Basically, her immune system was working against itself. She suffered from an autoimmune disease that prevented her body from digesting proteins. Every time she ate, it caused an allergic reaction inside her body. Her entire intestinal tract was affected and would swell with inflammation. This prevented her swallowing, and any food that made it to her stomach was unable to be digested, so she either vomited or had a bowel obstruction, diarrhea pain, and bleeding. Everything we had been doing to try to feed her was actually poisoning her. Her digestive system had shut down. She was essentially allergic to everything.

It didn't take long for us to realize that if you can't eat, you die, and our daughter couldn't eat. By that time, Hannah was three years old, but only the size of a nine-month-old baby. The pressure within our family mounted as we were forced to spend more and more time apart. Sleep deprivation, stress, and separation was normal. Ashley worked fulltime and took care of our boys who were still very young. I basically lived at the hospital with Hannah. Life became a juggling act; managing chaos was our specialty.

Time was running out for Hannah. We watched her life ebb away a little more each day. Besides being tiny, her hair became very brittle and began to fade and fall out. Each morning I found new piles of hair on her pillow until very little was left on her head.

Seeing pictures of Hannah a few months earlier with her pigtails still intact made me cry. I tried hard not to think about what the future would hold. Always having to deal with a current crisis made that relatively easy, until people began noticing how ill Hannah was and began asking questions. Then I couldn't hide from the ugly facts staring me in the face. It was no bad dream our family would wake up from.

Ashley and I never spoke aloud the reality that we lived every day, but we could see Hannah was dying. At the time, our silence was just a coping mechanism, for to speak something makes it real. Looking back, I see that our decision was significant. Only a year earlier, we buried our baby nephew, and the hurt was still fresh enough that I knew I could not dwell on it. Some probably thought we were denying the truth; I think we were denying a truth, not *the* Truth. I just knew I must not fall into a pit of despair, not while Hannah was still with us, so life went on.

During our crisis, Ashley and I began digging deeper into the Word of God. We knew that the answers to life would be found in that book, even if our experiences didn't always line up with it. We began listening to sermons in the evenings on one of the Christian radio stations we could pick up. We began reading the Bible more for ourselves (rather than just absorbing the Sunday sermons), and slowly we started to change. The more we read, the more starved of God we realized we'd been. Scriptures of Jesus ministering to others came alive to us. It seemed He loved and healed everyone He met. In the book of Hebrews, we found these words:

> Jesus Christ is the same yesterday, today and forever. Do not be carried away by all kinds of strange teachings.
>
> Hebrews 13:8-9 NIV

This verse really made me think. All of my Christian life, I attended church regularly and heard the same message regarding healing. "Don't get your hopes up. It's God who decides who gets healed and who doesn't." Even after I was healed of epilepsy, I still struggled with other conditions, like everyone else around me. I still had colds and allergies and such. I could see how this statement might be true; on the other hand, it didn't match up with what I was reading in the Bible. Somewhere I knew there was a discrepancy, and since Jesus was still on the throne, I figured that any inconsistency was happening on my end!

As I wrestled with this subject, I decided that just because my church didn't teach about healing, didn't mean it had passed away with the apostles. Even though healing wasn't a completely understood subject, it didn't mean it was not God's plan or His will. So I figured that healing had to be just as much for now as it was for when Jesus walked the earth.

Finally, the day came for us to make the long journey back to Great Ormond Street Hospital where Hannah was to have surgery to implant a feeding tube into her stomach. We had been through several excruciatingly traumatic attempts to fit a less invasive nasal gastric tube into Hannah's frail body and watched as each time she rejected it. This surgery was the last option for Hannah. There was no plan B, no medication that could treat her. The antihistamine, anti-allergy medication she was on, which was supposed to kill the autoimmune reaction, had caused an allergic reaction itself. Her body had gotten to the point that everything we put into it was treated as a foreign invader. Her immune system was stuck in overdrive, permanently attacking itself. Antibiotics, pain medications, food, even the adhesive in the medical-grade tape we used to keep IVs in place caused inflammation and bleeding.

The plan that we hoped would be a life changer for all of us involved Hannah being fed a synthetic formula called Neocate directly into her stomach. The formula was already broken down into amino acids in a way that her body could absorb. The formula was supposedly hypoallergenic, meaning that it was very unlikely that Hannah would react to it. We all knew this would not cure Hannah, but we were hopeful it would give us some time and give her some quality of life.

The night before Hannah's surgery, we stayed at my parent's home where we would leave the boys for a few days. We knew the drive to the hospital would take several hours, so my mom found a selection of dusty teaching tapes to help us pass the time. In the morning, we loaded Hannah and her little stuffed puppy dog into the car (puppy was having the same surgery as Hannah that day) and started up the tape player. In our collection were familiar sermons from Joyce Meyer and one from a preacher named Andrew Wommack. The title on the cassette was *Your New Identity in Christ*. It sounded interesting, so we picked it up and popped it in the player. Little did we know that the tape that had lain dormant in mom's drawer for over a decade was about to change our world forever.

As Hannah slept in her car seat, we listened to a squeaky American voice begin to unravel truths from the Scriptures. We both realized we'd never heard anyone speak like Andrew Wommack. He used so many verses, and every point he made was carefully backed up with Scripture. Some of his points were completely new to us, and I would have dismissed them immediately had he not proven them in the Word and had we not been in the midst of a crisis. For the first time in my Christian walk, I heard that God wanted us well, that healing was always His plan, that sickness was never from God but was a curse from which Jesus redeemed us. It all sounded too good to be true, but what if it was true? What if healing really was God's will? That would mean that Hannah could be healed! Ashley and I sat and listened, and listened again. It felt like we'd just been given a gold nugget and told where to find the mine. We needed to dig!

I determined in that car ride that I would explore these theories, and if there was any glimmer of truth in them, I would find it. Waiting in the hospital between pre-op tests, my mind mulled over the contents of that tape. I see now how important the timing of those events was. While I was thinking on godly things, my attention was pulled away from the seriousness of the situation playing out around me. I felt peaceful, even though nothing in our circumstances had changed. I was beginning to find hope and consider what life could be like if Hannah was well.

Eventually, the doctor came out with the test results. I could tell it wasn't good by the expression on his face. (Actually, they never shared any good news with us regarding Hannah's prognosis, so it wasn't a shock. But this time he looked more grave than usual.) "There's a problem with Hannah's blood results," he said. "Her blood is lacking the clotting factor."

Yet again, Hannah was one-in-a-million! Her blood's inability to clot was extremely rare, literally affecting one in a million people. As the doctor rambled, Hannah slept, blissfully unaware of the drama that surrounded her. It was then I remembered a picture the Lord had given me. I saw Hannah holding my hand as we walked together through green gates on her first day of school. I saw her riding a little red tricycle round and round our driveway, and I saw Ashley walking her down the aisle on her wedding day. Suddenly, it didn't matter what the doctor was saying; I knew that I was seeing the future, that Hannah was going to live!

"Uh-huh, yep, I understand," I lied. I really wasn't interested in listening anymore; my mind was focused elsewhere. I wanted the doctor to leave me alone so I could process my thoughts.

My mother-in-law sat with me as my backup while Ashley was working, so I shared with her some of the things I'd heard on Andrew's teaching tape. I wanted to hear her thoughts on it. She voiced many of the same concerns I had, "If healing is God's will, why isn't everyone healed? How do we explain why some people are healed and others aren't?" Though I didn't have the answers and I knew I could be setting myself up for more heartache, I figured false hope was better than no hope. I couldn't unhear the things Andrew Wommack said, and if there was any shred of truth to it, I wanted it.

To our great relief, Hannah's surgery went smoothly. The tube they attached in her stomach protruded through a small hole in her abdomen next to her belly button. There was a lot of tenderness, redness, and swelling at the incision site, and we had to keep it meticulously clean. Whenever we held Hannah, she would tuck her legs up to her chest to protect her tummy because it was painful when the tube caught on something or was knocked. The tubing extended about three inches from her stomach and needed to be taped to her skin, which was a simple process normally. However, the adhesive caused a horrible allergic reaction on Hannah's skin. It became raw and blistered and would itch and bleed. I was sure that our neighbors heard Hannah screaming each time we needed to change the tape and wondered what we were doing to our child.

After a few weeks post-op, we established a routine. It was much like bringing a newborn baby home for the first time; we were tired, bewildered, up every hour of the night, and relearning how to survive! Hannah never slept more than an hour without waking in pain or with wet sheets. Totally overwhelmed and sleep deprived, I sterilized medical equipment, prepared Hannah's formula, washed soiled sheets, and tried to keep daily life going. Child rearing, chores, and school happened regardless of how Hannah was doing. Bills still had to be paid; Ashley still had to work; and dinnertime still arrived every day.

When a couple of days passed vomit-free, it looked like we were finally on the right track. Hannah was still sore from the surgery, but she was keeping down the formula being pumped in through the tube. However, after a few weeks, her little body began rejecting the formula that was supposed to keep her alive. Her temperature spiked, and once again, the familiar symptoms of this horrible disease began to raise their ugly heads. Too weak to do much, our three-year-old who should have been full of life and energy, lay listlessly on the couch. Her body was unable to absorb the pre-digested formula, and her immune system was in overdrive trying to fight off what it saw as a foreign invader. Every drop of nutrition that we fed into her came out in one way or another. It was as if someone had pulled the plug on her life, and there was no energy left in her batteries to power up again. Her body, already severely malnourished, was literally fading away. The lights in her eyes dimmed and dark circles, the telltale marks of a body under attack, surrounded them.

Back we went to our regular hospital room, and the usual gaggle of med students in white gowns followed behind specialists like chicks following the mother hen. They didn't have to tell us; we already knew we were at the end of the road. There was no plan, no miracle drug, and no more time. But I again remembered the pictures the Lord had shown me: the little red tricycle, her first day of school, her wedding day. Somewhere inside, I tuned the doctor's voices out. I knew what they were saying, but it was like their words had no meaning. We had heard a different message—one of hope—from a God who was passionately in love with His children, whose healing power was alive and real; and somehow, somewhere, we had to find it for Hannah.

We wondered how healing worked for children who were not able to make decisions for themselves. None of the teachings we had listened to specifically mentioned praying for children. Ashley decided to check Andrew Wommack's website to see if he was ever in England, just so we could ask him how healing applied to kids. We knew of no one else who taught about healing or had experienced it. We felt that if we could just have a conversation with Andrew, we could reach what felt so close.

We knew it would take divine intervention to get Hannah released from the hospital at this point in the disease, but if Andrew ever came to England, we would at least know what to pray for! As Ashley scrolled though the dates on Andrew's website, he noticed a few international engagements, one of which was in England. In fact, it was the very next day!

There were a lot of questions yet to be answered, and more miracles were needed to clear a path to go to the meeting. But for the first time, I allowed my heart to skip a little happy beat. "This has to be God," we said. We began to pray for God to make a way where there seemed to be no way. The more we prayed, the more convinced we became that we needed to be at that meeting. It was probably a crazy and irresponsible thought to take our child to a place we did not know without a critical care team nearby and two other young children in tow, but we had nothing to lose and everything to gain. Hannah was going to die in a matter of days, and nothing the doctors could do would change that. We had to give God a chance. Crazy and irresponsible seemed our best option!

We made up our minds; when the doctors came in for rounds, we would do everything in our power to get Hannah released so we could make our pioneer journey north for the meeting. When the doctors herded in that morning, they looked grave. They started out as usual with their explanations of Hannah's lack of improvement, but then something happened that I know was God. Conversation turned mid-thought and one by one, the doctors began to agree that the best thing would be for Hannah to go home. There was nothing more they could do for her. Out of compassion, they suggested that we take Hannah home to live out her expected final seven days. "It's better for the family," they said, "if a child passes peacefully at home rather than in the clinical hospital setting." It must have seemed strange to them for parents to be excited to hear such news, especially when they were effectively giving out a death sentence.

We told them we were planning to see another specialist, and within a few hours, we were free to go (as free as a stroller, three car seats, and a truck full of supplies can allow anyway)! With Hannah loaded, we headed to the boys' school to bust them out. It was with great pleasure that I informed the unyielding school reception that I had come to collect my boys, and they would not be in school for the rest of the week. "No, I do not have permission from the principal," I said. "No, I'm not going to wait around to get it. The reason for their absence? We're going to be a family again this week!" It had been a long time since we had all slept under the same roof, and today was a day to celebrate. Of course, we were not sure exactly what we were celebrating, but it felt like it was going to be good!

While I gathered up the boys from their classrooms and the coats from the cloakroom, Ashley called our parents. We were counting on them being able to come with us on this adventure; we needed their help with the kids. It was rather unnerving to find out that none of them could join us. Without the security and safety net of grandparents, it would just be us and Jesus— but it was all part of God's perfect plan.

It seemed like everything we thought of, God handled. Sure, there were a few bumps and roadblocks, but the Lord went ahead of us and showed us the way around them. We called the number on Andrew's website to find out more about the meeting schedule and scout out the area. A lady named Kath at the venue where we were to meet reassured us that there would be enough children's workers to handle our needs, and it did not matter that we had not registered. The children's ministry at the conference would care for our four- and five-year-old boys, allowing us to concentrate on the message and take turns with Hannah. It was a huge relief to know that, and made us feel like we could survive this journey!

After a six-hour car ride and several long traffic delays, we arrived at the hotel late that night. We missed the first evening meeting, and the children were about to have a meltdown by the time we finally tucked them into bed. Despite being exhausted, I could not sleep. My mind was whirring in anticipation of the next day's events. Everything within me wanted to forecast the outcome. I wondered how we were going to get our family train moving again after such a late night. I even thought about what we might be able to find for breakfast. Yet in the midst of those everyday details, my heart dared to hope. Everything was riding on this great adventure. Life and death could be decided in a moment, and my heart wanted to rehearse that moment. Healing was God's best for Hannah. Of that, I was utterly convinced, and if it was His best then I was not planning to go home with a sick child.

The sun probably came up at some point that morning, but it was raining so hard it was difficult to see. I disliked rain. On rainy days, everything got wet, and rain and medical equipment don't mix. Throw in three children sandwiched into car seats, a stroller full of supplies that needed packing in the truck, pillows, blankets, favorite cuddly teddies, more blankets, snacks, coats, and activities, and you have several pairs of soggy shoes. Forget the thought of an umbrella; no one had enough hands for that with two small boys to hang on to (one of which has a reputation for disappearing).

Finally, with all onboard and every limb accounted for, our small but determined band of bedraggled pioneers arrived at the conference venue looking somewhat like a traveling circus. The car park was full by the time we arrived, but I was hoping for an umbrella-wielding attendant to help us unload our precious cargo. My silent prayer was answered as a smiley American guy greeted us with an umbrella.

Before long, the boys were dispatched to the children's ministry section, and we set up base camp at the back of the auditorium. Hannah was spread out in a nest we made on the floor, surrounded by various pieces of essential equipment and the DVD player. We set our minds to soaking up every last drop of the message and took shifts caring for Hannah, watching her silently slip away from us. After every session, there was a ministry time where the sick could receive prayer. Somehow, this always coincided with some type of medical or parental drama, which prevented us from getting to the front of the line before it closed. As time ticked by, desperation began to creep in. Saturday morning arrived, the final day of the conference, and Hannah was fading fast. She was limp and pale; she slept fitfully.

When her crying became so distracting that we retreated to the back room where the nursery convened, the mothers there took one look at her and swiftly exited the room until we were all alone. With just the three of us sitting on the carpet, and the video feed of the main meeting, I rocked my baby, trying to soothe her pain. In that helpless moment, I felt my guard slipping. I fought the thoughts trying to invade my mind. All the years of surviving were catching up with me. I was tired. My soul was heavy. I felt like my heart was going to burst. Had we come so far with such high hopes only to go home empty handed? Was the struggle to get this far all for nothing? Was this the end of the road for Hannah? Could she really die? I knew I couldn't let my mind go there, but the tears didn't listen. In all our years of struggle, I had not allowed myself to cry, determined not to open those floodgates in case I couldn't shut them again. But sitting on that floor, I suddenly came to the end of myself. All those months of bottled up emotions burst their carefully held boundaries until I was sobbing from the pit of my soul.

Then Lesley appeared. At the time, I had no idea what role Lesley played in the event organization, and I'm not sure what caused her to stumble upon us. But she joined us on the carpet, and the Lord used her to encourage us in the middle of our mess. She left us, and a few minutes later, she returned with Andrew and his wife Jamie. We were surprised he would take the time to meet with us, but I knew God was still working on our behalf. By this point in the day, Hannah had cried herself to sleep in her stroller, and we sat with Andrew and Jamie explaining the whole horrible story to them. We rehearsed her symptoms, her failed treatments, and her prognosis as we had many times to various experts. But this time something was different. When most people were faced with the grisly facts of Hannah's condition, they gave us looks of pity and sympathetic half smiles, but not Andrew. He looked right back at us and said, "Well, that's a piece of cake for Jesus!" His boldness spoke volumes to us. He had a quiet confidence that told me he really believed what he was saying. His words were founded in faith, not superficial encouragement.

Something dropped into my heart in that moment. Peace settled over me and answered my questions. Jesus gave us authority over all diseases—including the one that was attacking Hannah's body. We didn't even have to fight a battle; we simply needed to vote. Just like our government works from majority votes, this spiritual issue of life and healing did too, and Jesus plus me equaled a majority (not to mention Ashley and Andrew and Jamie and the rest of our family)!

As Andrew and Jamie prayed with us, inside I knew that we were praying the Word of God concerning healing, and if we believed it was done then it didn't matter what it looked like, our actions would reflect whatever we believed. When Andrew and Jamie left, my mind raced ahead to how this healing thing would work out. What would it look like? We already had two healthy children, so I settled in my heart that we needed to treat Hannah just like we did our sons. Ashley and I talked about what to do with the feeding tube and how to begin feeding a child who had never eaten solids. Should we begin with something easy to digest and gradually introduce new foods, as if she were an infant? Should we wean her off her medications? What about the pump she was connected to 23 hours a day?

As we pondered these things, Hannah woke up, and we broke the exciting news to her that while she was sleeping, Jesus had healed her. Without skipping a beat Hannah said, "I want to eat French fries and ketchup; I want McDonald's." Coming from a child who had always associated food with pain, we could see the power of marketing was very evident in her life! The rest of our questions were resolved shortly thereafter, thanks to the wisdom of our five year old. Ashley went to collect the boys from the children's ministry area to explain to them what had happened to Hannah. Both boys were excited, especially Zachary. He piped up, "Now Hannah is better, and she'll be able to eat anything. She won't need her tube anymore, right Dad?" What could we say to that? He was right; either Hannah was healed or she wasn't. And if she was, then everything Zach just said was true! Nothing about Hannah looked different after she was prayed for. She still looked pale, still had dark sunken eyes and patches of scarecrow-like hair. Yet in simple childlike faith, we looked past her outward appearance and did what came naturally; we headed to McDonald's!

One hour of every day, we unplugged Hannah from her pump. For that little bit of time, Hannah could move around without dragging a little cart along behind her, and we could act like a regular family. The time would always go quickly though, and we could tell, without checking our watch, when her hour of freedom was nearly over: Hannah would physically begin to fade. It was as if she were being deprived of her energy supply, like a battery-operated toy slowing down as it nears its point of recharging, and it was time to plug her in again. But on this day, something different was about to happen.

It had been at least thirty minutes since her "unplugging" when we gave up looking for a McDonald's in that strange town and finally settled on KFC. As I opened the car door, out popped Zach (a big boy, now that he could unbuckle himself) followed closely by Joshua, and then Hannah looking like a critter that had just been sprung from a trap. She held my hand tightly, and we walked together across the parking lot. Then it hit me, she was walking! She had the energy to walk, and she wasn't even plugged in! It had been a long time since I had walked along with my three year old when she wasn't riding on the base of an IV stand or being pushed in a stroller. Inside, we all sat opposite Hannah staring as she worked her way through different items on the menu. She chewed and swallowed each bite of fried chicken, French fries, corn, ice cream, yogurt, and brownies carefully. The entire menu was open for anything she wanted to try. I'm sure onlookers thought we were horrible parents letting our kids eat dessert first and then just standing by watching as they bounced around the restaurant full of sugar, but we enjoyed every minute of it!

As the hours passed, we never did plug Hannah back into her machine. It was not all "smooth sailing" though. We had opportunities to doubt, opportunities to consider her disease returned. Later that afternoon, in fact, the telltale symptoms reared their ugly heads, like a final battle cry. Hannah coughed. She coughed again. Soon she was coughing and choking. The boys ran for cover, but Ashley and I were ready. We had been given a taste of normalcy, and we were not backing down. Jesus *had* healed Hannah, so we prepared for the counter attack.

Symptoms, we have since discovered, have a common pattern of reappearing after a person receives healing. It is so easy to be moved by them and allow fear to creep in, but we must stay alert to the devil's sneaky tricks. Like anything else that belongs to the enemy, it flees when the light is shone upon it.

As Hannah began to choke, Ashley took authority and simply commanded those symptoms to stop in the name of Jesus. And they did. They had no choice. We knew the disease left Hannah's body when we prayed. We knew what we were now experiencing was only a lie—a chance for fear to empower disease to regroup and attack Hannah again. Two days later, we took Hannah back to the hospital where we had basically lived with her for over a year. It was wonderful to see the look of utter disbelief on the nurses' faces as we walked with Hannah into the hospital ward. The child they had sent home to die was not only still alive, but thriving! Hannah's doctor took us straight into his office and examined her. He was at a loss for words.

"How can I describe what has happened to your daughter," he stumbled, "other than to say this is a miracle." We told him "miracle" was just fine, so that's what he wrote in his notes! He dismissed us from the hospital that same day. From then on, Hannah was known to the medical staff as the "miracle girl!"

Nine months later, the hospital agreed to remove the surgically implanted feeding tube, which had not been used since Hannah was healed. The wait was worth it though, when Hannah's final pre-surgery blood tests came back showing the clotting disease she was previously diagnosed with was also gone. The last words I heard from her doctor were ones I'd longed for her entire life—and ones I know I will never forget: "Hannah, we have checked you out, and we can't find one thing wrong with you. You are perfect!"

five

JESUS—OUR FAITH EXAMPLE

One of the most important understandings for any believer to have is that there is only one savior, and we are not Him. Christ is our savior. He is our perfector. He is the miracle worker. He is the healer. And it is only by His life working in and through us that others experience the goodness of God. However, we cannot will people into God's Kingdom or force them to receive healing. Quite the opposite. Although Jesus was the propitiation for all mankind, each person has to individually accept His sacrifice for himself. Just as we cannot receive salvation or healing on behalf of another, neither are we held responsible for whether or not they receive the truths of Scripture or God's provision.

Faith is important. Faith is how we access the promises that God's grace has provided. While healing is only one of the many provisions included in His grace (John 1:16), we must remember that whether or not a person receives from God is not based on us. The Bible says:

For it is God who works in you both to will and to do for His good pleasure.

Philippians 2:13

…who through faith subdued kingdoms, worked righteousness, obtained promises, stopped the mouths of lions, quenched the violence of fire, escaped the edge of the sword, out of weakness were made strong, became valiant in battle, turned to flight the armies of the aliens. Women received their dead raised to life again…

Hebrews 11:33-35

Faith is a byproduct of our relationship with God. When Jesus ministered, He provoked faith in those He ministered to. He wanted to see what *they* were believing for and who they thought He was. He needed to know what they thought He could do for them. When people came to Jesus, He questioned them or got them actively involved in what He was doing by telling them to "stretch out your hand… go your way… show yourself to the priest" (Matthew 12:13, Mark 10:21, Matthew 8:4). Their active participation ignited faith within their hearts and allowed Jesus to do amazing things in their lives.

According to Jesus, people receive in accordance with how they believe.

Go your way and **as you have believed** let it be done for you.

Matthew 8:13 (emphasis added)

And when He had come into the house, the blind men came to Him. And Jesus said to them, "Do you believe that I am able to do this?" They said to Him, "Yes, Lord." Then He touched their eyes, saying, "**According to your faith** let it be to you."

Matthew 9:28-29 (emphasis added)

And throwing aside his garment, [Bartimaeus] rose and came to Jesus. So Jesus answered and said to him, "**What do you want Me to do for you?**" The blind man said to Him, "Rabboni, that I may receive my sight." Then Jesus said to him, "Go your way; your faith has made you well." And immediately he received his sight and followed Jesus on the road.

Mark 10:50-52 (explanation and emphasis added)

Jesus never forced God's will of healing on anyone. He always worked according to their faith. Once, Jesus approached a man at the pool of Bethesda who had been sick a very long time. He asked, "Do you want to be healed?" (John 5:6). What if the man had said no? I believe the Lord would have left him there. Why? Because He didn't care? Absolutely not, but because He cared enough to not violate that person's will.

What if someone doesn't have faith? According to Scripture, we have all been given "the measure of faith."

For I say, through the grace given unto me, to every man that is among you, not to think of himself more highly than he ought to think; but to think soberly, according as God hath dealt to every man the measure of faith.

Romans 12:3 KJV

I am crucified with Christ: nevertheless I live; yet not I, but Christ liveth in me: and the life which I now live in the flesh I live by the faith of the Son of God, who loved me, and gave himself for me.

Galatians 2:20 KJV

Scripture clearly states that we all have the ability to believe. It also says we have the faith of Christ in us. None of us lack in the area of faith; we do not need more faith. Rather we need to ensure that our minds are not consumed with doubt and unbelief.

The Bible shows us examples of faith in action, all of which can be classified as active or passive faith. Active faith means that an individual's faith causes them to reach out and take what they know is theirs, without the help of a prayer minister or anyone else bolstering them. In Scripture, we see that the woman with the issue of blood who crawled through the crowd to touch Jesus' garments had active faith (Mark 5:25-34).

Another example from Scripture of active faith is the story of the Centurion's servant. In Matthew chapter 8, we see his servant healed because of his faith. The Centurion didn't need Jesus to lay hands on his servant; he knew his servant would be healed solely because of Jesus' word (Matthew 8:5-13). Jesus says this type of faith is "blessed" (John 20:29).

For a person with passive faith, it takes all they have to overcome unbelief and receive. These people generally do not understand God's true character. They often know God can heal, but do not know if He will heal them. These people usually need someone (a prayer minister, friend, or pastor) to come alongside them in faith and encourage them to receive.

An example of passive faith is found in Mark chapter 9. In this story, the father of an epileptic boy came to Jesus and said, "If you can do anything... please help" (Mark 9:22). This man did not know if Jesus would have compassion on his son. He did not know if it was possible for his son's suffering to end. This man was struggling with doubt. Jesus did not immediately dismiss this man because of his unbelief though. He encouraged the man with the truth.

> Jesus said to him, "If you can believe, all things are possible to him who believes."
>
> Mark 9:23

The scripture says, "Immediately the boy's father exclaimed, 'I believe; help me overcome my unbelief!'" With Jesus' help, this father recognized his unbelief and came to a place of faith so Jesus could minister to his boy (Mark 9:14-27).

Belief is the primary form of faith. As we mature, we learn to use our faith to receive from God for ourselves. Those new to faith or young in the Lord often receive healing based on the faith of others, but it is their own relationship with the Lord—their own faith—that is necessary for them to stay healthy. As ministers, we need to meet people where they are (without condemning them for not being more mature), and allow the Holy Spirit to grow them in faith. Jesus showed us how to do this.

Compare Jesus' encounter with Jairus (from Mark 5) with that of the Centurion we already read about. When Jesus met Jairus, his daughter lay dying. At Jairus' request, Jesus went to his house to lay hands on the girl and heal her. Jesus did not tell Jairus it was unnecessary for Him to come. He did not say, "All I have to do is speak, and she'll be made well." He met Jairus at the point of his faith and went to his house as asked (Mark 5:22-24, 35-43). The result in both Jairus' and the Centurion's story was complete healing.

Of the people who believe that God wants to heal or provide for their needs, many understand they need faith to receive this provision. Many more confess that they are "in faith," and yet are obviously struggling. A greater number still do not have a clear understanding of what faith actually is, even though they claim to be "in" it. There seems to be a discrepancy in the body of Christ of what faith is. According to Hebrews 11:1, faith is defined as:

> Now faith is confidence in what we hope for and assurance about what we do not see.
>
> NIV

> Now faith is the assurance (the confirmation, the title deed) of the things [we] hope for, being the proof of things [we] do not see and the conviction of their reality [faith perceiving as real fact what is not revealed to the senses].
>
> AMP

I believe many people confuse faith with hope. Hope can be defined as wishful or positive thinking. It is the feeling that what is wanted can be had or that events will turn out for the best. Notice it is a feeling. Hope wants the best but doesn't really know if it will happen. This sounds exactly like what I hear people say when they come forward for prayer. "I'm waiting on God," they say. But faith is more than this.

Faith is the substance of hope. There is evidence associated with faith when there is none with worldly hope. Biblical hope, however, is the birthplace of faith; it is an expectation of good. If you hadn't first hoped that the Gospel was true or that God was real, you would not have been able to pursue a relationship with Him to receive salvation. But faith goes further than hope. Hope ignites our imagination to believe; faith germinates and receives the harvest of belief.

A simple definition of faith is "trusting confidence." Faith understands that everything in the Word of God is ours for the taking. Faith delivers the confidence we need to step out on those promises and act according to them. Faith is something we have *now*; it is not something we wait for.

All believers have faith (Romans 1:17). Without it, we couldn't please God (Hebrews 11:6) or be saved (Ephesians 2:8). Without faith, we perish (Deuteronomy 32:20), but with faith, we inherit all God promised us in His Word (Hebrews 6:12). Faith is powerful!

For whatever is born of God overcomes the world. And this is the victory that has overcome the world—our faith. Who is he who overcomes the world, but he who believes that Jesus is the Son of God?

1 John 5:4-5

Faith is confident and single minded. It does not consider worldly alternatives.

Because of faith also Sarah herself received physical power to conceive a child, even when she was long past the age for it, because she considered [God] Who had given her the promise to be reliable and trustworthy and true to His word.

Hebrews 11:11 AMP

Faith can be seen!

Some men came carrying a paralyzed man on a mat and tried to take him into the house to lay him before Jesus. When they could not find a way to do this because of the crowd, they went up on the roof and lowered him on his mat through the tiles into the middle of the crowd, right in front of Jesus. When Jesus **saw their faith**, he said, "Friend, your sins are forgiven."

Luke 5:18-20 NIV (emphasis added)

Faith is both a noun and a verb. We see evidence that we possess it through actions. When Jesus ministered, He saw each person as an individual and followed the Holy Spirit's leading to minister differently each time. As ministers, we need to learn to follow Jesus' example. He was our greatest model of faith in action! We must remember to see the person asking for prayer, not just their problem. Just as each person is unique, the way we minister to them should be Holy Spirit guided, not formulaic.

Just like a gardener knows when fruit is ripe for picking, the Lord knows which hearts are open to receive. A gardener does not decide which fruit ripens. He wants it all to come to maturity, but he knows how to spot a ripe one! I clearly remember the first time I recognized this. During worship one Sunday morning, I was praying in tongues and heard the Lord say, "This lady has faith to be healed today." *That's nice*, I thought, hoping it was just passing information, not instruction. But as worship continued, the message burned inside me until I couldn't think about anything else. I began studying the back of the lady's head whom God had pointed out to me and couldn't help but notice she was wearing hearing aids in both ears.

And so the bargaining with God began. "Lord, I really don't know this woman. This is weird. Is that really You talking to me, or did I eat something funky?"

I finally agreed to pray for the woman on the condition that God make it really obvious that she was the one that He meant had the faith to be healed. Sure enough when worship ended, the pastor asked us to greet someone new. The lady I was wrestling about in my mind, spun around and looked at me with a huge grin. Knowing if I didn't take my chance now, I would chicken out, I blurted, "The Lord told me that you have faith to be healed today. Can I pray for you?"

"Oh yes," she said like she was totally expecting my blast of information. One speedy prayer later, and she removed both hearing aids. Her deafness was healed!

Not only was this a lesson to me about being bold and stepping out regardless of my flesh, it showed me how easy it is to minister to people when we rely on the Lord to lead us. The Holy Spirit knows who is ready to receive, and He will show us if we listen. It's almost like cheating!

True faith can also be heard. A person's speech is often the first indicator of their faith—or doubt. Jesus said, "Out of the abundance of the heart the mouth speaks" (Matthew 12:34). What a person believes eventually makes itself known (2 Corinthians 4:13), but our belief can be changed! Romans says, "Faith comes by hearing, and hearing by the Word of God" (Romans 10:17).

When people hear the truth of God's Word about healing, salvation, etc., faith rises in their souls. But that faith must have an outlet. It needs to be spoken.

> So Jesus answered and said to them, "Have faith in God. For assuredly, I say to you, whoever says to this mountain, 'Be removed and be cast into the sea,' and does not doubt in his heart, but believes that those things he says will be done, he will have whatever he says.
>
> Mark 11:22-23

Words are powerful (Proverbs 18:21). Every time we are subjected to the words of others, we have to choose how they will impact us. When we hear a negative report from the doctor or belittling words from our family, those words have the power to create our reality.

Jesus gave us an example of how to respond to word challenges when He was tempted by Satan in Matthew chapter 4. When Satan tempted Jesus, Jesus did not counter him with physical might, nor did He summon legions of angels to fight on His behalf. Jesus countered him with the Word of God. When we understand all that Jesus accomplished for us on the cross, the Bible says that we overcome our situation and Satan's attacks by the "word of our testimony" (Revelation 12:11).

As believers, we have the power to create or destroy with our words. Just imagine what could happen if we started using our words to speak life! We would become bold (Proverbs 28:1) and release the power of God in our situation.

> For You have magnified Your word above all Your name. In the day when I cried out, You answered me, And made me bold with strength in my soul.
>
> Psalm 138:2-3

> So shall My word be that goes forth from My mouth; It shall not return to Me void, But it shall accomplish what I please, And it shall prosper in the thing for which I sent it.
>
> Isaiah 55:11

God has inscribed His Word—Jesus—on our hearts. Our job is to agree with what's in our hearts by opening our mouths and speaking His Word (Jeremiah 31:33). My daughter showed me how to put this principle in action after a long day of playing on the beach. It came to that dreaded moment no young child liked when you have to shake the sand out of your shoes and go home. With much whining and gnashing of teeth, we began to gather our belongings. It was then we discovered that a shoe was missing.

Unfortunately, it wasn't just any shoe; it was Hannah's favorite blue jelly shoe with the dolphin on the bottom. Apparently, her left shoe had floated away unnoticed. Like any good parents, we broke the news of the loss to Hannah and braced ourselves for the onslaught of emotion typical from our three year old in these types of situations. Without flinching Hannah said, "It will come back in Jesus' name." Being that those blue jellies were the only pair of shoes we had for her on vacation, we buckled down to spending the next day searching for a replacement pair of size six jellies.

After walking the mile-long promenade and scouring every beach souvenir store we could find, we gave up. We could not find one pair of shoes in Hannah's size. With the lone dolphin shoe still attached to her foot (because she refused to remove it), we returned to the beach the following day. We spent another great day splashing and playing about the waves and sand. But as we were leaving, something blue caught our eye.

Sure enough, it was Hannah's missing shoe! Hannah nonchalantly picked it up as if it were exactly where she thought it should be, buckled it on, and said, "This one has been on an adventure!"

While it sounds like a cute childhood story, for us it was a powerful lesson in faith. Hannah simply believed that Jesus was big enough to bring back something that was important to her. Her uncomplicated, child-like faith had convinced her that He loved her, so why wouldn't He bring back her favorite shoe?

It is easy to become overwhelmed and discouraged when circumstances don't look good. Rather than using our words to agree with the situation in front of us, the Scriptures say we can change the outcome (Matthew 17:20). Hannah spoke out what she believed and did not move from it until she saw it happen. In today's world, we want to microwave our miracles, but Hebrews 6 says that "through faith and patience, we inherit what is promised" (Hebrews 6:12). Patience is not a popular message, but it's amazing what a difference three days can make! Let me encourage you to keep standing on the promises of God, keep speaking the Word only, and call those situations that "be not" right now "as though they were" what the Lord intended them to be (Romans 4:17).

In its simplest definition, faith is confidence in God—confidence so strong it can be felt. I remember being home alone with the children while Ashley was at work. Out of the blue, there was a knock at the door. As I walked towards the door to open it, I felt a boldness rising up on the inside of me. I opened the door an inch to see who was there, when it was suddenly forced open by a strange man on the other side. He was angry and shouting and threatening me.

Later we found out that a man we fired because we discovered he was stealing from us and lying, went to some local loan sharks to whom he owed money and gave them our address as a place they could collect the money owed them. As the man at the door explained (in great detail) what he would do to us unless we paid, I could hear my three babies playing in the next room. Out of nowhere, I felt a boldness rise up inside of me and words began to fly out of my mouth. I'm still not sure what I said, but I remember the effect. With every word I spoke, the man recoiled as if I punched him. Eventually, he stumbled back down the garden path and clung to the fence post with a terrified look in his eye. He took off running down the street while I stood on the doorstep not quite sure what had happened. As I closed the door behind him, I melted into a heap on the floor and reached for the phone to call Ashley. The boldness I felt in that moment was way beyond my natural feeling or ability. God supernaturally moved in my heart, and the effects spoke for themselves.

Faith is not magical. It is a powerful, tangible force that often shows itself as confidence and boldness. People who live by faith are in constant communication with God and tend to be happier, healthier, more confident, and positive people. They live above the circumstances of life. This is not to say that life is easier for these people; it's just that people of faith respond differently to crisis and rise above life's challenges because they have confidence in God.

When people are truly convinced that God loves them and that He will act on their behalf, perfect peace flows out of their lives. The peace these people experience surpasses understanding (Philippians 4:7). They experience no turmoil, anxiety, or fear regardless of their circumstances, but instead rest in a quiet confidence of God's goodness.

> There is no fear in love; but perfect love casts out fear, because fear involves torment. But he who fears has not been made perfect in love.
>
> 1 John 4:18

Being confident of this very thing, that He who has begun a good work in you will complete it until the day of Jesus Christ.

Philippians 1:6

Faith changes how we respond to everyday situations. After Hannah was healed, we began to realize that the power of God that we had through faith could change our circumstances and situations. Everyday obstacles became faith projects for us.

I noticed there were still areas in my life where I had learned to live with problems that were not God's best. I began asking myself how far I was willing to believe God. I had seen God heal major diseases in both my own body and my daughter's, yet I still struggled with less serious conditions. It didn't make sense to me. As I meditated on this, my mind went back to the moment Hannah was prayed for. I realized that either this healing thing was real and God could be trusted, or it was a lie. I realized I had to choose to either believe or not. And I discovered that if I really believed, it would show in my actions. Did I have actions that showed my belief? What about my orange allergy?

I'd had an orange allergy since I was child. My entire life had adapted to compensate for it. In comparison to some of the other things I dealt with, it was a minor condition but still potentially life threatening. Just a few weeks earlier, I had been at a friend's house vomiting with inflamed skin after touching one of her tables. She didn't know about my allergy and had recently cleaned the dining table with an orange, oil-based cleaner. I thought of everything I did to ensure no orange prod-ucts ended up in our home. Not only did my allergy eliminate oranges and orange juice from my family's diet, but I never used orange, oil cleaning products or lotions either. It suddenly hit me that God's promises covered every detail of my life, and I didn't have to live with second best any longer—not even in regards to allergies. "I believe it!" I shouted, standing alone in my kitchen. I couldn't wait for Ashley to get home from work so I could tell him what happened to me that afternoon.

The minute he walked through the door, I explained what the Lord had showed me and asked him to pray with me. I wanted to try my new healing out, but there was nothing in my house to test it on! The next day I went to a Bible study. When refreshments were passed, I grabbed a cup of coffee and piece of carrot cake. "Wait Carlie," my friend cautioned. "That one has orange juice in it!"

"Oh good," I said. "Give me a big slice; I want to test out my new healing." My friends thought I was crazy, but I was con-vinced God had healed me, and I was not going to be talked out of eating that cake. It was good! And I have been eating oranges without any problems ever since.

From then on, the way we responded to sickness in our house changed. It's not that sickness never came calling again, but we learned not to tolerate it. We despise sickness as much as sin; we don't want it in our lives in any form. Even if cold symptoms start creeping up, we get mad. How dare the devil try to make us sick! We are the temple of the Holy Spirit. Satan does not have permission to mess with our bodies!

Any time we're faced with a challenge or a bad medical report, the rubber of our faith meets the road. Are we going to choose to believe the truth of God's Word? Are we going to follow Jesus' example and believe by fighting the good fight of faith with our words? Let us choose wisely, that we may live the life God intended for us (Deuteronomy 30:19).

Six

THE POWER OF IMAGINATION

Imagination is a powerful force. The ability to "see" spiritually is important in all areas of receiving, but it is especially necessary in healing. When we use our imaginations for the good that God intended, we connect our brains to the reality in our spirit. Our spirit is full of the Spirit of Christ (Romans 8:9). It is 100% saved, healed, prosperous, and wise even though our body is not.

> And if Christ is in you, the body is dead because of sin,
> but the Spirit is life because of righteousness.
>
> Romans 8:10

In order for our bodies to reflect the truth of who we are in the spirit, we must be able to accept what we cannot physically see by faith. But God in His goodness, has given us help to do that. He has given us an imagination.

When the prophet Jeremiah was beginning his ministry, the Lord appeared to him. During this encounter, Jeremiah was terrified, not just of the awesomeness of God, but of the calling itself. Jeremiah didn't feel worthy to be a prophet. He didn't feel equipped, so the Lord had to show Jeremiah how He saw him.

> Moreover the word of the Lord came to me, saying, "Jeremiah, what do you see?" And I said, "I see a branch of an almond tree." Then the Lord said to me, "You have seen well, for I am ready to perform My word."
>
> Jeremiah 1:11-12

I'm sure when God asked Jeremiah what he saw, Jeremiah wasn't standing in an almond grove. He saw with his imagination. As the Lord encouraged Jeremiah, "You have seen well," Jeremiah's picture of himself began to change. *Maybe I can do what God has called me to,* he may have thought. All we know for sure is that Jeremiah began to prophesy.

Just like Jeremiah, in order for us to change what we see outside, in our circumstances, we must first change our picture inside. When our thoughts change, our feelings will follow. James explains how this works negatively saying, "When desire has conceived, it gives birth to sin; and sin, when it is full-grown, brings forth death" (James 1:15), but we want to use it positively.

> If people can't see what God is doing, they stumble all over themselves; But when they attend to what he reveals, they are most blessed.
>
> Proverbs 29:18 MSG

Aside from seeing yourself as healthy in the future, there comes a point when healing needs to be revealed in your life *now*. Picturing the healing process as you pray helps. Maybe you visualize warm oil flowing through your body or imagine pain lifting off your body. Maybe like I did, you picture switching off sickness, or picture tumors shrinking, or ear canals opening like a floodgate on a river. Ask the Holy Spirit to show you what is happening when you pray, and engage your imagination.

While your imagination is engaged, speak to your mountain (Mark 11:23). If your thoughts begin to wander and focus on symptoms and circumstances, act swiftly. Take authority over minor symptoms before they escalate; do not give the enemy a foothold. It is easier for your heart to believe the Word when situations first arise than down the line as unbelief creeps in. Fear mounts over time if it is entertained, but you have the ability to identify and eliminate it with the truth of God's Word. Let's go back to Jeremiah's example:

> Then the word of the Lord came to me, saying "Before I formed you in the womb I knew you; Before you were born I sanctified you; I ordained you a prophet to the nations." Then said I: "Ah, Lord God! Behold, I cannot speak, for I am a youth." But the Lord said to me: **"Do not say**, 'I am a youth,' For you shall go to all to whom I send you, And whatever I command you, **you shall speak. Do not be afraid** of their faces, For I am with you to deliver you," says the Lord. Then the Lord put forth His hand and touched my mouth, and the Lord said to me: "Behold, I have put My words in your mouth. See, I have this day set you over the nations and over the kingdoms, to root out and to pull down, to destroy and

to throw down, to build and to plant." Moreover the word of the Lord came to me, saying, "Jeremiah, **what do you see?**" And I said, "I see a branch of an almond tree." Then the Lord said to me, "You have seen well, for I am ready to perform My word." And the word of the Lord came to me the second time, saying, "**What do you see?**"

Jeremiah 1:4-13 (emphasis added)

What we say is very important. Proverbs says death and life are in the power of our tongue (Proverbs 18:21). That's why when Jeremiah spoke unbelief, the Lord jumped in and stopped him. While our confession can be used to change our situation for good, sometimes we need to hold our tongues to keep from spewing out words of unbelief.

Words are a major culprit of unbelief, fear, condemnation, guilt, offense, and self-doubt. Words overpower us when we receive them into our hearts and dwell on them. Left unchecked, these words can grow into a forest of weeds in the garden of our hearts. Again, an effective weapon against evil words is our imagination. Visualizing yourself plucking out the seeds of these words before they can germinate and grow roots will keep them from developing into trees that block your view of God.

Be strong and of good courage, do not fear nor be afraid of them; for the Lord your God, He is the One who goes with you. He will not leave you nor forsake you.

Deuteronomy 31:6

The only weapon Satan has is deception. He is a master at magnification. That old saying, "turning a molehill into a mountain," comes from him. Satan spends most of his time trying to convince believers that they are sick, poor, defeated, worthless sinners. He tries to tell them that their circumstances are God's will or that God could heal them, but they don't deserve it. He says, "You are the reason that you are sick," and "If you take a headache pill then you're not in faith." When facing his lies, it's important that we know he cannot tell the truth (John 8:44) and that condemnation is never from God (Romans 8:1).

Using the weapon of our imagination will help us experience change regardless of our past results. Past experiences can dictate our future if we let them. However, Paul tells us to "forget those things that are behind and press on to what lies ahead" (Philippians 3:13). That is good advice! How do we do that? By faith.

God has called us into faith, not fear. The writer of Hebrews says, "Now faith is…" (Hebrews 11:1). Faith is a present tense verb. It is made for now, not yesterday or tomorrow! Nothing we can do will change our yesterdays, and Jesus said our tomorrows have enough worries of their own (Matthew 6:34). Faith is made for today. "But I want my tomorrows to change," you say. Here's the good news, faith can affect our future, but only after we use it to change our today!

We can practice faith, just like a doctor practices medicine. We will not do everything perfectly all the time, and that's okay. Otherwise, why would we need Jesus? But if we guard our tongues and refuse to focus on the problem by confessing and speaking the Word only, we will see our situations change.

Healing is a fruit of our relationship with God, but there is no fruit without root. By seeking the Healer, we find healing and all the other aspects of His character.

> As His divine power **has given to us all things** that pertain to life and godliness, **through the knowledge of Him** who called us by glory and virtue, **by which have been given to us exceedingly great and precious promises, that through these you may be partakers of the divine nature,** having escaped the corruption that is in the world through lust.
>
> 2 Peter 1:3-4 (emphasis added)

Let me throw out a disclaimer. Part of living in a fallen world means that we will have plenty of opportunities to exercise our faith. Practice using your faith on your own body. Start with everyday grumbles, aches and pains, and colds. Even David fought the lion and the bear before he fought Goliath (1 Samuel 17:36). Gaining victories in the small areas will build your faith and help you to gain confidence before ministering to others. This is how we prepare for war in times of peace. No one wants to run into a battlefield without the appropriate armor and weapons!

> Now to Him who is able to do exceedingly abundantly above all that we ask or think, according to the power that works in us.
>
> Ephesians 3:20

His power at work in us can do far more than we dare ask or imagine.

CEV

Part of our armor is not limiting God. We can limit God by thinking healing (or any other promise) can only manifest in a particular way. God has hundreds of ways of ministering and getting His grace to us if we are open to Him.

A few years ago, Hannah and I waited in the rain for her brothers to come streaming out through the gates of their school. Hannah's legs swung back and forth in her hot pink stroller, and a cup of dirt lay nestled in her lap. The dirt contained a seed she had planted in nursery school that morning. With no sign of the seed, Hannah's grubby little fingers clutched her muddy cup, careful not to spill the precious cargo she had spent so much of the morning planting.

Like most days, Miss Maxine waited next to us. Noticing the cup in Hannah's hands she asked, "What's that Hannah?"

"A bean plant. We growed it at school today."

"That sounds like fun," she said. "Are you going to plant it in the garden?"

"No, we are going to eat it," Hannah replied. "We are going to have beans for dinner tomorrow!"

Maxine raised her eyebrows and let out a little chuckle. "Hannah," she said, "if that seed grows beans by tomorrow, I'm going to have to believe in your Jesus!"

An act of God surely would be the only way that pot of mud would ever produce a bean plant, especially by the next day!

But Hannah did not blink in the face of Maxine's astonishment when she said, "Jesus can do it. Can't He Mum?"

"That's right," I replied.

Maxine had been watching our family closely over the past year. She was intrigued by our faith and had seen Hannah recover instantly from a life-threatening condition weeks earlier. It was persuasive evidence, but now the little girl everyone thought would be dead was talking to her about a Jesus who could grow a bean seed overnight. As ridiculous as it seemed, Maxine didn't immediately dismiss what Hannah said.

At home that afternoon, we carefully set the pot on the window ledge in the kitchen and gave it some more water. Every so often, Hannah would climb up on a chair to peek inside the pot to check on the plant's progress. At bedtime, she decided it must be sleeping because there was still no sign of it poking through the soil.

The next morning at breakfast, the toast popped, the kettle boiled, lunches were packed, faces cleaned, teeth brushed, and crumbs swept before we noticed that Hannah's little bean seed had grown. Really grown! A twelve-inch beanstalk stood in the little pot, leaning precariously to one side. We had to use a pencil to stake it up and keep it from falling over.

"Mummy," Hannah shouted, "we can have beans for dinner!" As of yet there were no signs of beans on her new plant, but after the growth of the night before, I was not about to disagree.

At school that afternoon, Hannah could not wait to find Maxine and tell her about the beanstalk. Maxine decided to come home with us and see this amazing plant for herself. All the way home, our tribe of children talked about eating beans for dinner. I too was curious to see what that bean stalk had been doing while we were away!

Only Hannah walked into the kitchen without shock written on her face. The plant had grown so tall it was touching the ceiling and three long green beans were dangling from it! Maxine's jaw dropped, and her eyes widened. She fell backwards into our kitchen chair and said, "I believe in your Jesus, Hannah!"

You see, God is not limited by our natural rules or circumstances. He is ready to meet us at the point of our faith! For many people, that means receiving healing gradually. For others, it means believing for instantaneous healing when someone lays hands on them and prays. Wherever we decide to extend our faith, He is there!

When Zach was about seven years old, he had an earache. After the fourth day of using prayer like Tylenol, (every four hours when the symptoms returned), I asked the Lord what was going on. He said to ask Zach, so I did. Zach said he wanted me to take him to see the doctor. He said that if he saw the doctor, he would be better. I was a little disappointed. I wanted our family to handle sickness "by faith," but I made the appointment.

The next day we went in to see the doctor. Zach sat opposite him and told him that he had had an earache in both ears, but Jesus had already healed one. He only wanted the doctor to look at the other one that was still hurting. The doctor seemed a little surprised but took his torch and peered into Zach's ear, "Yes," he said, "you have an infection. You'll need some medicine."

As we walked out of the doctor's office, I asked Zach how he was feeling. He informed me that he was all better since he had seen the doctor. Sure enough, when we got home, we discovered the fever he'd had for four days was gone. Zach never did take the medicine. He set his faith that if he saw the doctor, he would be healed. So that's the point at which he was able to receive. Adults do this too, but the truth is we can receive our healing instantaneously if we are willing to believe it!

Are you ready to believe God for healing? How far are you willing to take your belief? Are there areas in your life where you could trust God more? Healing must start with you. Does that mean you can't pray for someone else until all your physical ailments are gone? No. But it does mean you must decide to believe and confess the Word above your circumstances. It does mean you must settle the issue of fear in your own heart and learn to harness your emotions. It also means you need to take the necessary steps to capture your negative thoughts. Will you be successful all the time? Probably not. Renewing your mind is a process, but you must start the process! Regardless of where you are in the process, God can use you. However, it's nearly impossible to give away something you are not convinced of.

Seven

CULTIVATING THE MIRACULOUS

Can we prepare our hearts to receive from God? It sure is easy, when things aren't going the way we think they should, to become frustrated and angry. It's easy to find ourselves doubting God and siding with the opposition! But if we desire to see the power of God manifest in our lives, there are conditions in which that power is cultivated.

Not long ago, I learned this the hard way. One rainy afternoon in a city exactly like mine, a husband (actually, my husband) committed the unpardonable sin of forgetting that his wife is always right. Feeling the injustice and looking for a way to pardon the offense, I retreated to the bedroom to complain—I mean pray.

When I eventually quit whining, I realized the Lord was quiet. He did not respond to my whining, so I tried crying. When that didn't work, I asked the Lord to fix that man He gave me. But still I heard nothing. My pity party began to feel rather lonely. Finally, after the tears had run dry and the Kleenex were soggy, I listened. In those next few moments, I heard the Lord say, "Let's talk about you."

In His most gentle way, the Lord told me about all of the good things He had put inside me. He refused to discuss the wrongs of another with me because His love covers a multitude of sin (James 5:20). As I wrote down the things He told me, joy and peace exploded in my heart. My situation had not changed, but I had.

> You will keep him in perfect peace, whose mind is stayed on You.
>
> Isaiah 26:3

I learned an important lesson that day. My thinking produces fruit. The entire time that I focused on the bad, the wrong, the hurt, my thinking took a downward spiral. Anger, frustration, and turmoil played with my emotions. Yet when I chose to spend a few minutes mediating on the truth of God's Word, my heart was freed of that pain.

> And you shall know the truth, and the truth shall make you free.
>
> John 8:32

> For to be carnally minded is death, but to be spiritually minded is life and peace.
>
> Romans 8:6

What we choose to meditate on affects our emotions and produces fruit in our lives. Our thinking directly impacts our ability to receive the good things the Lord is trying to get to us. If we want to taste the good stuff, we have to plant good seed.

> Finally, brethren, whatever things are true, whatever things are noble, whatever things are just, whatever things are pure, whatever things are lovely, whatever things are of good report, if there is any virtue and if there is anything praiseworthy—meditate on these things.

> Philippians 4:8

Keeping our mind stayed upon the Lord, plants good seed. You can often tell the type of seed people have planted by the look on their faces and the words that they speak. There's always a telltale, lemon-sucking expression that gives it away! The Bible tells us that the joy of the Lord is our strength (Nehemiah 8:10). That joy is also one of the first things the enemy tries to steal from us when we allow ourselves to be distracted by the junk around us. The great thing is, if we don't like the fruit in our lives, we get to pray for a crop failure and replant!

Be encouraged. The Lord has uniquely planted in you gifts, talents, ability, and purpose that positions you for victory. Life may give you lemons, but you don't have to suck them! Start agreeing with God's promises, and watch the fruit of them grow in your life. You can receive every good thing He has planned for you!

But you need to be aware of common weeds that tend to grow in the garden of our hearts. A common "weed" that trips us up when we are believing for a miracle or breakthrough is offense. When offense comes, we need to uproot it immediately.

Allowing weeds to grow in our hearts sucks the life out of our gardens and hinders the growth of healthy fruit. The nature of a weed is to ultimately take over the whole garden, strangling the life out of otherwise healthy shoots.

The gospel often offends people. It is the power of God unto salvation for all who believe (Romans 1:16). But this very prerequisite often offends those who would rather remain passive in their faith.

> Jesus answered and said to them, "Go and tell John the things which you hear and see: The blind see and the lame walk; the lepers are cleansed and the deaf hear; the dead are raised up and the poor have the gospel preached to them. And blessed is he who is not offended because of Me."
>
> Matthew 11:4-6

Faith is not meant to be passive. Rather than sickness producing pity, sympathy, and helpless defeat, a revelation of the love of God sparks righteous anger in the heart of a believer over that sickness. It shouts "faith!" at an intruder attempting to steal, kill, and destroy a child of God by trespassing in the temple of the Holy Spirit. Healing, like salvation, is not automatic. When we respond to God's wonderful provision in faith, this paves the way for His miraculous power to flow through us. Unfortunately, most people spend half their lives trying to get something from God that He has already given them!

The kingdom of God operates by a faith system. Jesus said, "All things are possible for him who believes," (Mark 9:23). We cannot receive what we are unwilling to believe. Faith looks not at natural experience or circumstances but into the unseen spiritual realm where God is. By placing more value on spiritual than earthly things, we elevate faith and allow God to work in our lives.

Jesus himself was bound by the law of faith. No matter how many people Jesus healed or how varied their circumstances were, the one common ingredient they all had was faith. In one instance, the Word says that Jesus entered a town but could not do many mighty miracles because of the townspeople's lack of faith (Matthew 13:58). Even Jesus could not override people's unwillingness to believe.

When we refuse to believe what God's Word clearly says, it is called unbelief. I once heard a minister say that unbelief believes in "un." "Un" is the opposite of God. It lifts circumstances—what we can see, hear, taste, and smell—above God's Word and causes those things to become reality in our lives.

For as he thinks in his heart, so is he.

Proverbs 23:7

Unbelief causes us to be offended, and it limits what we can receive from God. The trouble is that it's easy to get tangled up in unbelief. As humans, we tend to look at natural, physical things to tell us facts rather than spiritual truth.

Romans 8:6 says, "to be carnally (fleshly) minded is death, but to be spiritually minded is life and peace" (explanation added). We have all the faith we need to overcome anything thing life throws at us, however, our faith can waiver depending on our focus. Unbelief divides our hearts and creates fear.

If any of you lacks wisdom, let him ask of God, who gives to all liberally and without reproach, and it will be given to him. But let him ask in faith, with no doubting, for he who doubts is like a wave of the sea driven and tossed by the wind. For let not that man suppose that he will receive anything from the Lord; he is a double-minded man, unstable in all his ways.

James 1:5-8

Unbelief and fear are often partners in crime that counteract our faith and are definitely something we want to uproot when preparing our hearts to receive from God. Fear is the enemy of faith. People fear different things: pain, death, poverty, change. Fear may even raise its head as insecurity. Someone may not feel worthy to receive from God or may fear the rejection of others if they stand in faith (pressure from loved ones to follow medical advice or fear of disappointing their doctors). That is why, as ministers longing to share our testimony with others, we must have a solid foundation—the Word. Only truth can set us free, but only the truth we know can help us overcome these obstacles to our faith. Remember, faith works by love, and perfect love casts out fear (Galatians 5:6 and 1 John 4:18).

Praying in tongues is an effective way to overcome fear and unbelief. Praying in tongues "builds us up in our most holy faith" (Jude 20). When we pray in the Spirit, we not only build faith, we build endurance. Many people never experience God's best because they quit too soon. Typically, people look to their body or circumstances to tell them if they are healed or if their miracle has been provided. Often if they do not see an instant difference, they become discouraged and think, "It doesn't work!" But the Word says:

> Do not become sluggish, but imitate those who through
> faith and patience inherit the promises.
>
> Hebrews 6:12

It is important to encourage ourselves first with the Word, guard our tongues, and not dig up the seed of faith planted in our hearts by confessing everything that is wrong with life. Just like a farmer must have patience to allow the seed he planted to grow through the processes of germination and harvest, we must not give up on faith, but allow it to work miracles in our lives.

Another hindrance to our faith is self-centeredness. When we become focused on ourselves, it is easy to overlook the goodness of God displayed in our lives. Trauma and disappointment can act like blinders that, when undealt with, skew our perception and cultivate a victim mentality that consumes the heart. The fruit that self-centeredness generates limits us because, by its nature, it is a work of our flesh: depression, neediness, and negativity that is constantly sowing gloom and doom. Just as nature produces after its own kind, so does this victim mentality. When we believe and confess that everything in our lives is bad, everything is someone else's fault, or there is nothing we can do about it, this becomes a self-fulfilling prophesy, trapping us in a cycle of "bad luck."

Our emotions are God given. We were created to be feeling and sensual beings, but we are still able to control these emotions. After all, self-control is a fruit of the Spirit. Unrestrained emotions can cause damage to us and those around us like a landslide gathering momentum. I know that for me personally, in those times when I have allowed my emotions to run away from me, they have ended up running over me! Since graduating from the school of "it's all about me," I can see my own self-centeredness manifesting in an unthankful attitude, unbelief, pride, and laziness. While not a pretty lesson to learn about yourself, it has been an important one for which I am grateful. The Word says that people perish for lack of knowledge. (Hosea 4:6) This "knowledge" is not intelligence or knowledge in a worldly sense, but a knowledge of the things of God. When people have little understanding or knowledge of what the Word says or of Who God is, they naturally rely on worldly understandings and experiences that they have learned and observed.

For example, my parents and I did not receive Christ until I was well into my teenage years. I was raised with good morals but lacked any real knowledge of God. When challenges came my way, I handled them to the best of my human ability. God never factored into my responses, even once I was born again. It took time for me to read and learn about the promises of God. It took time for the Word to become real in my heart and for that knowledge to become reality in my actions.

My own confessions showed evidence of this lack of knowledge. For as long as I can remember, those around me commented, "Carlie catches everything that goes around." I heard it so often, it became a part of who I was. I was always sick. Every month, I had a cold or flu or some new ailment. I began repeating it myself: "I seem to collect diseases!" I had no idea that I was cursing myself with my own words.

Proverbs says:

> My son, attend to my words; incline thine ear unto my sayings. Let them not depart from thine eyes; keep them in the midst of thine heart. For they are life unto those that find them, and health to all their flesh.
>
> Proverbs 4:20-22

If the lack of knowledge causes us to perish, it makes sense that an abundance of it will bring us life (3 John 1:2). Practically, this means we have to spend time discovering the truth. What God says about us and our situation is truth, and it has the power to change the way we think and speak. Scripture calls this "taking our thoughts captive."

> For the weapons of our warfare are not carnal but mighty in God for pulling down strongholds, casting down arguments and every high thing that exalts itself against the knowledge of God, bringing every thought into captivity to the obedience of Christ, and being ready to punish all disobedience when your obedience is fulfilled.
>
> 2 Corinthians 10:4-6

In short, "taking thoughts captive" means weighing each one as it comes to see if it lines up with what God says. If a thought doesn't match up, it needs to be corrected with the truth. For example, if someone believes, "I'm not worthy; I don't deserve to receive healing," that's a lie. If healing was somehow based on our goodness or on our performance, no one would ever be healed—not even those in the Bible. Nothing we receive from God is based on us; it's based on what Jesus did.

I remember a lady who requested prayer for a brain tumor. She was in the last stages of cancer and had to be pushed in a wheelchair by her concerned family members. Unable to speak clearly or hold her head up, she came hoping for a miracle. I could sense the family's desperation as they told me her long, sad story. I was reminded of the time Jesus prayed for the little girl and asked the relatives to stand outside (Mark 5:36-43). I knew this family was terrified of losing their mom and that their fear was overwhelming her faith. Asking them to take a seat at the side, I knelt down on my knees until I could look the mom right in the face. She was barely conscious.

I didn't know what to do, so I began to pray in tongues. As I listened to the Holy Spirit, He showed me that this woman felt unworthy to receive healing. So I began to minister to her with the love of God. I began telling her just how special she was, how much God loved her, and what a wonderful plan He had for her life. I told her she was precious—God's own special treasure, set apart and holy. I told her that God didn't want to see her suffer, that He wanted to see her well and free from cancer. A tear gently rolled down her cheek. I asked her if anything was stopping her from receiving her healing. She lifted her head, looked at me, and clearly said, "I'm not worthy."

"That's a lie," I told her. "Jesus made you worthy. Are you willing to accept that?" She nodded, so I asked her, "Would you like to go for a walk then?" She smiled, and I took her by the hand. Together we stood. She walked free of the wheelchair and into freedom from cancer!

There is another "C word," other than cancer, that if allowed to grow can be just as damaging. Condemnation. Often people think, *I brought this on myself; I just have to live with it.* Even if this was true, God's grace is sufficient, and He is the rescuer of our souls! Our stupidity, ignorance, or poor choices do not disqualify us from receiving God's love, forgiveness, and promises; only we can do that!

I remember praying for an elderly gentleman confined to a wheelchair. He was well into his 80s, but his mind was still very sharp. He wanted prayer but didn't feel he deserved it because his emphysema was caused by years of smoking.

Because his breathing was so bad, he lived on an oxygen machine. But once he understood that God's grace was available to him, he took off his oxygen tubes and decided not to live with that condition any longer. He got angry at the devil when he realized he'd believed a lie and had been robbed of years of freedom and health. I asked him to do something he couldn't do before without oxygen, so he went for a walk. Soon he was laughing.

Apparently, he also had curvature of the spine (I didn't notice this while he was sitting in the wheelchair), and when the power of God touched his lungs, it also healed his spine. With a straight spine, he became a couple of inches taller, and now his pants were too short!

Being the author of lies and having had many years in which to develop them, Satan has spewed no shortage of them. He likes to tell people, "God sent this sickness to teach you something. It's not always God's will to heal; if nobody ever got sick, then nobody would ever die." All these lies produce unbelief and rob us of our miracle. How do we know they are lies? They produce death rather than life, and Jesus came to give us life (John 10:10). These toxic thoughts can be prettied up, but they are still weeds that will not produce good fruit. When thoughts of unbelief spin out of control, the best thing to do is refuse them permission to land!

Life happens whether we are ready for it or not. Everyday circumstances develop and continue without our input. People speak, act, and change; governments rise and fall; life starts and stops, all outside our control. Often the moments we can't control disturb us most. They replay in our minds while we lay awake at night trying to switch off our brains and sleep. It's frustrating, but truthfully, we will never be able to control everything around us. The only things we can learn to control are our thoughts. We can become the air traffic controllers in the airports of our lives!

The realization that I could control my thoughts was never more real to me than in the moments when life hung in the balance. The points when I'd had so many seizures, I needed to learn to walk again; when the doctors said our unborn baby was deformed and offered us the option of termination; when our child was given one week to live; when we were sued and it looked like we would lose everything; when thugs threatened to burn down our house; when we lost loved ones; and when life hurt so bad, it was hard to breathe. In those times, our survival depended upon our ability to hear the voice of God above the chaos.

Then the Lord used an airport to show me how to control my thoughts to hear His voice. Visualize an airport control tower with planes circling overhead. Each time a plane approaches the tower, it radios the tower controller for permission to land. Without the go-ahead from the control tower, no plane has the authority to land at the airport. Our thoughts are like planes. Some planes are loaded with blessing, while others are full of toxic waste! We cannot stop the planes from coming into contact with the tower of our mind, but we do not have to give them permission to land!

We can literally recognize and isolate our thoughts to judge whether they are good, bad, or ugly (2 Corinthians 10:5). The best way to do this, is with God's Word.

> The thief cometh not but to steal and to kill and to destroy. I am come that they might have life, and that they might have it more abundantly.
>
> John 10:10 KJV

> But the fruit of the Spirit is love, joy, peace, longsuffering, kindness, goodness, faithfulness, gentleness, self-control. Against such there is no law.
>
> Galatians 5:22-23 KJV

> Finally, brethren, whatever things are true, whatever things are noble, whatever things are just, whatever things are pure, whatever things are lovely, whatever

things are of good report, if there is any virtue and if there is anything praiseworthy—meditate on these things.

Philippians 4:8

Do our thoughts bring fear or dread? Then they are from the enemy. Are our thoughts true? Are they of good report? Do they fill us with love, joy, and peace? Then they are likely of God. If we discover a thought circling our tower that's not good or of God, then all we have to do is refuse it permission to land and replace it with one that does. This amazing ability enables us to control our emotions, our air space, and takes us one step closer to receiving the promises of God!

Now to him who is able to do immeasurably more than all we ask or imagine, according to his power that is at work within us.

Ephesians 3:20 NIV

Sometimes, the weeds that ensnare believers are tied to wrong doctrine, ignorance, or legalism. Each of these perversions of thought can hinder the way we relate to the Lord and cause us to misinterpret Scripture and make wrong judgments.

For indeed the gospel was preached to us as well as to them; but the word which they heard did not profit them, not being mixed with faith in those who heard it.

Hebrews 4:2

The Word without faith profits nothing. It becomes just words without any real meaning, and our relationship with the

Lord becomes sterile, mundane, ordinary, and powerless. Without a clear understanding of God's Word and what it means to be a child of God, we can begin to look to other things to shape who we are. We look to our job, family, money, education, ability, performance, all kinds of things. These issues cause many people to misunderstand the true nature of God. They often relate to God the same way they relate with others.

Past hurts, if left untended in our hearts, can propel us towards self-reliance rather than Christ-dependence. Self-reliance causes a negative self-image and usually makes receiving from God difficult. For healing to take place, it is crucial that we let go of any performance-based Christianity and embrace our new identity as children of God.

This is amplified when someone has been sick for a long time. Their lives and thoughts are affected. Family dynamics, finances, decision-making, household responsibilities and daily life all change as a person learns to live with a chronic condition. Long-term sickness creates a new identity for them that doesn't line up with their identity in Christ. I know this was certainly true for me! It is often difficult for chronically sick people to remember being well, and that lack of positive imagination hinders them from receiving from God. When you have been prayed for many times but never have any results, the false hope and disappointment take a toll. After a series of disappointments, it is hard to drum up expectancy. Faith is stifled and hearts can become hardened to God's goodness (Proverbs 13:12).

A hardened heart is a dangerous thing. Not only can disappointment cause it, but so can persistent unbelief, disobedience, hatred, unforgiveness, bitterness, envy, and strife.

For where envy and self-seeking exist, confusion and every evil thing are there.

James 3:16

It takes a period of time to develop a hard heart. The Bible describes the process as a heart waxing gross (Matthew 13:15 KJV). Just like a candle is formed by layer upon layer of wax, a hardened heart is developed by repeated rejections of God's truth. A hardened heart often signals a withdrawal from God, and it hinders how people can receive from Him. Hearts that have become hardened are generally unthankful, sceptic, negative, angry, resentful, or rebellious. They find it difficult to experience joy and therefore, gravitate towards pessimism. But like any other obstacle of faith, the Word of God overcomes!

For the word of God is living and powerful, and sharper than any two-edged sword, piercing even to the division of soul and spirit, and of joints and marrow, and is a discerner of the thoughts and intents of the heart.

Hebrews 4:12

For the weapons of our warfare are not carnal but mighty in God for pulling down strongholds.

2 Corinthians 10:4

So how do we begin to prepare our hearts to receive from God? How do we weed the gardens of our hearts and cultivate the miraculous? That's easy! The truth sets us free (John 8:32)! But we first have to know the Word.

At the conclusion of this book is a series of confessions. These are tools to help you begin the process of cultivating right thinking. These confessions are comprised of everything good God thinks about you with corresponding scriptural references. As you read the confessions, put your name in there and agree with them. Start to see yourself as God sees you. You are amazing, the apple of His eye (Psalm 17:8)!

eight

EVERYDAY MIRACLES

Several years ago as I was meditating on scripture, I asked the Lord where miracles came from. He said, "The bridge to miracles is found in the secret place." *That was cryptic, but okay.* Then He led me to read Psalm 91, which begins:

> He who dwells in the secret place of the Most High God
> shall abide under the shadow of the Almighty.

If we desire to see more of the power of God working in our lives through signs and wonders, we must live in the secret place of an intimate relationship with Jesus Christ. We can't just visit once in a while. Letting our relationship permeate every part of lives will have dramatic effects; I know it has in my life.

The natural outflow of living in the spirit and receiving the things of God is our desire to share it. Jesus said to "go into all the world and preach the Gospel (good news) to every creature" (Mark 16:15). As we've discussed before, that good news includes the healing of our bodies. Children naturally imitate their parents. Their behaviors, mannerisms, accent, actions, thought patterns, and decision making are all shaped through the formative years they spent abiding together. As children of God, created in His image, heirs to the kingdom, and filled with His Holy Spirit, it is part of our nature to imitate our Father. Just as naturally as earthly children imitate their earthly parents, we too will begin to imitate the Lord as we abide with him.

Miracles are conceived in us and through us as we dwell in the secret place of the Most High. Through relationship with Him, we get to partake of the great and precious promises that bring the dead back to life, heal the crippled and diseased, set the mentally ill free from their torment, and break every chain life tries to bind us with (2 Peter 1:2-4). This miracle of relationship is not one that can be microwaved; it takes time, a life-long journey, but it can start today! The truth is that mighty works begin in our hearts through everyday conversation with Jesus.

In a farmhouse long ago, on a rainy afternoon, I decided to bake a pie. This activity doesn't sound particularly spiritual, but everyone was out and about, and I had a rare moment of alone time to do something creative. So the pie baking commenced and filled the house with glorious aromas of yumminess. I set the pie on top of the stove to cool while I checked emails. Our three farm cats, a.k.a. the mousers, assembled themselves around me to stare at the moving images on the computer screen and periodically trample across my keyboard.

In my journey with Jesus, I had recently discovered that small talk was as equally important in my relationship with Him as it was in any earthly relationship. Hearing God in the little things, learning to tune in to His still small voice for direction and following it was training ground for me to believe for bigger things. Sometimes life got busy, and taking time to develop my spiritual ears was a new adventure.

However, as I pecked away at the keyboard that afternoon, the last thing that I thought I would hear the Lord say was, "The cat is eating your pie!" It sounded so off the wall that I did what most people do. I ignored it. The three cats were sitting next to me, all present and accounted for, and certainly not eating my pie. After the third time hearing that message, the thought inside me was so loud that I looked around and decided to get a visual of my pie just to be safe.

As I headed into the kitchen, there on the stovetop was a cat—eating my pie! Greater than the shock of finding a strange cat in my kitchen eating my pie, was the realization that God, the Creator of the universe, was so in tune with my life that He took the time to speak to me about a pie, and I could hear Him!

The truth is that we can all hear God all of the time. He is constantly thinking about us and talking to us.

My sheep hear my voice, and I know them, and they follow Me.

John 10:27

Why is it important to be able to hear God's voice? For many reasons, but mostly because He knows the way ahead. He knows us, our future, and the path that will most fulfil our hopes and dreams. The Holy Spirit leads us into truth, shows a way of escape in times of danger, reveals our future and purpose, convicts and teaches us, opens doors of opportunity for us, and loves us with an everlasting love.

This ability to hear God was made more real to me that day of the pie fiasco, but I didn't realize how important it would prove to be until a few days later. I was driving down a hedge-lined, country lane taking our children to school when I heard inside me, "Brake!" This time, I didn't question it. I immediately stomped on the brake, and out of a hidden farm gate, another vehicle shot in front of me. We would have collided at 60 mph if I had not stopped when I did. Listening to the Lord that day probably saved our lives.

Small talk is a powerful part of developing an intimate relationship with Jesus. Take the time to talk about the little things. It is amazing what we will hear when we take time to listen.

Be still and know that I am God.

Psalm 46:10

As we develop our spiritual hearing, not only does it transform our lives, but it becomes much easier to pray for other people, too. Intimacy with Jesus causes us to see people differently, to look for the good in them, and to see them through His eyes rather than as a bundle of problems. Everyone is different and uniquely created by God. When we love people as He loves them, we become an extension of God's hand—ministers of reconciliation moved by compassion.

Compassion is a powerful force; it is love that compels us to act. Every time that Jesus was moved with compassion in scripture, miracles followed. Ask the Lord to help you see each person who comes to you the way He does. His love never fails. There are not many things in this world that we can say never fail, but God's love never fails because it is a perfect, no strings attached, unearned, undeserved, crazy, extravagant, and ever-lasting. His love both created us and cures us. It crushes fear in a heartbeat, and it's in us!

One of the most dramatic deliverances from fear I ever witnessed that came through a move of compassion was at a meeting in Phoenix, Arizona. A young man came to ask for prayer for his wife. She was upstairs in their hotel room, too sick to come to the meeting. She had been bedridden with a crippling condition that left her in constant pain and unable to move for years. No doctor had been able to help her.

The young man asked me to agree with him in prayer for his wife's healing, but as I listened to the Holy Spirit, I felt that he needed ministering to as well. So I began with him. The Holy Spirit showed me that this young man was dealing with fear. Together, we took authority over fear and spoke peace over him. As he allowed the peace of God to rule in his heart, God's perfect love drove out fear, and tension drained from his face. He left buoyant and happy.

Later that evening, I saw the man again. This time he was accompanied by a beautiful young woman. I didn't recognize him immediately (I had seen a lot of people by that point), but he reminded me that I had prayed for him that morning. He looked so different; his countenance completely changed. He wanted to come back and share his testimony with me. He said, "On the way back to my hotel room, after you prayed, something happened to my wife. When I walked into our room, she was sitting up and completely healed." She said that the power of God came upon her suddenly as she lay in the bed. All pain left and strength returned to her body.

He went on to tell me how his wife had been longing to step out in faith and believe God for healing, but his fear had kept them both in bondage. He was terrified of losing her, and every time she wanted to step out in faith, he became more afraid because it meant no medicines, no doctors, and possibly no life. But the moment God's love penetrated his heart and the fear left him, she was able to receive too. No one spoke to her. No one touched her or prayed for her. But the power of God was released, and she received. I still don't totally understand how it worked, but I know that the compassion of God flowing through me into her husband was the catalyst that enabled her to receive.

Another side effect to hanging out with Jesus is boldness. This may sound odd, but let's think this through for a minute. Jesus is crazy in love with us. His perfect love casts out fear. If the Lord of the universe is on my side and thinks I'm amazing, who cares what anyone else thinks about me or what the world throws at me? Victory lives in me! Fear cannot remain where loves resides. While I'm thinking upon Jesus rather than my circumstances, I begin to get excited because now I see challenges as an opportunity to overcome rather than as a crisis. I begin thanking God ahead of time for my coming break-through before I even see it. *Boom!* My faith becomes effective because now I'm focusing on every good thing that is in me in

Christ Jesus (Philippians 1:6). Boldness, confidence, and faith abound. I'm moved with compassion in response to the Holy Spirit inside me. Now the power of God is able to flow through me, transforming not just me but those around me.

> Now when they saw the **boldness** of Peter and John, and perceived that they were uneducated and untrained men, they marveled. And they realized that they had been with Jesus. And seeing the man who had been healed standing with them, they could say nothing against it. But when they had commanded them to go aside out of the council, they conferred among themselves, saying, "What shall we do to these men? For, indeed, that a notable miracle has been done through them is evident to all who dwell in Jerusalem, and we cannot deny it.
>
> Acts 4:13-16 (emphasis added)

We can be bold about the promises of God! It's not our job or our reputation on the line to see the promises fulfilled. It's His. (And God is not in heaven worrying that He won't be able to deliver!)

During a mission trip to Nicaragua, the team I was leading visited a school on the island of Ometepe. Through the bustling crowd of excited children, a sweaty little hand tugged at my shirt. I motioned for the team to follow me, announcing that we were going to watch God do something amazing. We followed the little girl to a plastic chair in a sea of people. In the chair sat another little girl with one leg considerably shorter than the other. She couldn't walk properly and had to sit and watch as the other children played. Her mother sat next to her on the ground. Taking one look at the little girl's plight, it was obvious what needed to happen. I turned to the team and said, "Watch this everyone; Jesus is going to grow out her leg!" I couldn't believe the boldness coming from my mouth.

I looked at the little girl and gently lifted her legs straight out in front of her. Immediately, the short leg popped out level with the healthy leg. I didn't even pray for her! She jumped off the chair grinning from ear to ear and took off running while her mother sat weeping. Neither of us could speak one another's language, but the joy was evident, and words were no longer needed.

We may be the only representation of Jesus a person ever sees. We may even be the first person to ever tell someone that they can be healed. Healing, like other signs and wonders, opens the door for people to experience the goodness of God. It is the goodness of God that leads man to repentance (Romans 2:4), and that is the biggest miracle!

Miracles are easy for Jesus and should be part of our everyday lives as the "greater works" He assigned to us (John 14:12). Yet children usually grasp this quicker than adults because they simply believe that God will do what He said He would. I love praying for children; they don't think up all the reasons why faith won't work for them!

Years ago, while ministering at a conference in London, Ashley and I met a young family whose son was struggling with autism. Despite their difficult situation, the family exuded joy and thankfulness.

When they approached Ashley and me, the first thing they mentioned was the healing of our daughter Hannah. They told us how much it encouraged them before explaining how their son, Daniel, then seven, was diagnosed with autism and couldn't speak. It was evident as they spoke that much of their lives had been taken over caring for Daniel's special needs. They asked us to pray for him, so we sat down in a quiet corner and asked the Holy Spirit how to pray for Daniel.

The Holy Spirit told us to give the parents a nugget of truth, a starting point. He showed us that the boy's condition had been going on for such a long time that seeing a complete healing would be overwhelming for the parents, so we started small. I asked, "What are you believing for? What change would you like to see right now?" (Bite size miracles are easier to swallow sometimes!)

They explained that if Daniel could talk, it would make a huge difference in their lives. It would eliminate some of his frustration, and it would allow him to go to a regular school. Speech would improve his behavior and help him form relationships and express emotions.

Together, we agreed in prayer and laid our hands on Daniel's head. We simply prayed and commanded his brain to function normally. Shortly after the prayer, Daniel's parents began talking with us. In order to include Daniel, I asked, "Daniel, what do you want to be when you grow up?"

Daniel looked at me and said, "I want to be a doctor!"

Awestruck, his parents just listened as he began communicating normally like any other boy his age. The more we all talked, the more we realized just how smart he was. "Daniel, I think you'll make an excellent doctor," I said.

The Bible says, "We walk by faith, not by sight" (2 Corinthians 5:7). In other words, we walk by what we know rather than by what we see with our natural sight. But what happens if we pray for something or someone and nothing happens? Be patient. Remember, things may be working that we cannot see. When Jesus cursed the fig tree in Mark 11, He knew that His words immediately went into action, but the disciples didn't until they saw the tree wither from the inside out (Mark 11:12-24). They were only looking at the outside condition of that tree; they did not consider what power was at work inside of it. No matter what we see (or don't see), never counteract words of faith with those of unbelief. Be encouraged that the Word is working away in areas unseen and continue to believe.

> And we desire that each one of you show the same diligence to the full assurance of hope until the end, that you do not become sluggish, but imitate those who **through faith and patience inherit the promises.**
>
> Hebrews 6:11-12 (emphasis added)

It's natural to look at what we see or feel and use that information as a measure of success. But this is not faith. Faith says, "I know I'm healed. Jesus paid for my healing, and I receive it." Unfortunately, most people say they will know they are healed when they feel it in their body. Then they spend time wondering why they still feel sick. We want to move beyond this place to faith that is not moved by what it sees, to a place of bold assurance that comes from spending time with Jesus.

A young lady once approached the prayer line I was in during a ministry training session. She was completely deaf from birth and read lips to communicate, but she wanted to receive her hearing.

The woman I was training joined me in prayer. As we laid hands on the young lady, I knew we would see this victory first by faith. I explained to the young lady what was going to happen when we prayed. I told her that the power of God would be released through our words and would go into action immediately to open her ears.

We prayed and spoke life to her ears, but nothing much seemed to happen. I could tell by the look on each woman's face that they were a little disappointed. I encouraged the young lady that the Word of God was indeed working in her body and that it would continue working effectively if she would believe. As the young lady walked away, my companion looked crestfallen; her face could not hide her emotions. I reminded her of the lepers who met Jesus and were healed as they went (Luke 17:11-19). I encouraged her to check in with the young lady the next morning and expect to see a difference.

The next day my trainee, Pam, saw the young lady we had prayed for. She was on the far side of the parking lot entering church. Pam called out to her, and the young lady turned around as she heard Pam call her name. Her ears opened in that moment, and she could hear perfectly! Praise Jesus that patience had its perfect work in her!

God loves us so much! He will use whatever He can to get His grace to us. We don't have to believe perfectly or have all the right doctrines. We don't have to be spiritual giants; we just need simple faith. Remember it's Jesus who is the power source; we are only the vessels that His power flows through to touch others (John 15:1-8). If we can go with the flow, He can get the job done!

Miracles are easy for Jesus. He will get the good stuff to us through whomever will cooperate with Him—man, beast, donkey, child or even an adult! One Sunday, Ashley and I were teaching children's church about the prophets of Baal. Strangely enough, Zach, our son who was eight years old at the time, was actually listening! At the end of the teaching, we led the children in a prayer of salvation. Afterwards they practiced listening to God by ministering to one another.

The next day at school, Zach had an interesting conversation with Joe, a boy in his class. Joe was a troubled child, disruptive and rude. Zach and I had often talked about him and his behavior. We talked about his need for a friend who would never leave him—a friend like Jesus.

That day at school, Zach reached out to Joe. "My God is more powerful than Pokémon, and if you come outside with me at recess, I'll prove it!" That was a challenge Joe could not pass up, so he followed Zach to the field at recess.

"This is like a competition," Zach said. "Whoever wins, their God is the most powerful. I will build a pile of sticks, and you build a pile of sticks. If the birds come and pick up your sticks, then Pokémon is powerful, but if the birds come down and pick up my sticks, then my God is real and more powerful!" Joe agreed, and the boys began collecting sticks.

"To make my pile of sticks harder to find, I covered it with leaves," Zach told me. "I was gonna ask God to come down and set fire to them, but I figured I would get in trouble, so I just covered them instead."

It never occurred to Zach that his theology was based on an Old Testament principle or that God might not send birds to get his sticks. I asked Zach what happened, and he said, "The birds came and picked up my sticks. That showed Joe that our God is bigger than Pokémon!" Who would have thought to use a pile of sticks and some birds to lead someone to Jesus? Whatever it takes, right?

God is ready to show Himself strong through believers. He will move through us in ways that we have never considered if we will just open our hearts and minds. Amazing miracles happen when we take God's promises at face value—straight from the book—and act on them, rather than looking for reasons why they won't work for us (Mark 9:23).

The biggest miracle is that of eternal life. Someday soon, you may have the opportunity to lead a person to Christ. Be prepared for this—it's the most important prayer you can pray! Salvation is a free gift available to everyone. All we have to do is believe and receive.

If thou shalt confess with thy mouth the Lord Jesus, and shalt believe in thine heart that God hath raised him from the dead, thou shalt be saved. For with the heart man believeth unto righteousness; and with the mouth confession is made unto salvation....For whosoever shall call upon the name of the Lord shall be saved.

Romans 10:9-10, 13 KJV

There is no set way to pray for salvation, but it could sound like this:

Jesus, I confess that You are my Lord and Savior. I believe in my heart that God raised You from the dead. By faith in Your Word, I receive salvation now. Thank You for saving me!

As His children, our loving heavenly Father has another gift He wants to give every believer. This gift is the supernatural, miraculous power we need to live our new lives in Christ and keep hold of all His promises—including healing. It is the power of the Holy Spirit.

For everyone who asks receives, and he who seeks finds, and to him who knocks it will be opened. If a son asks for bread from any father among you, will he give him a stone? Or if he asks for a fish, will he give him a serpent instead of a fish? Or if he asks for an egg, will he offer him a scorpion? If you then, being evil, know how to give good gifts to your children, how much more will your heavenly Father give the Holy Spirit to those who ask Him!

Luke 11:10-13

Therefore I say to you, whatever things you ask when you pray, believe that you receive them, and you will have them.

Mark 11:24

Here is an example of a prayer you can pray to receive the baptism of the Holy Spirit:

Father, I recognize my need for Your power to live this new life. Please fill me with Your Holy Spirit. By faith, I receive Him right now! Thank You for baptizing me. Holy Spirit, You are welcome in my life.

No matter what you or the person you're praying for is dealing with, it's a piece of cake for Jesus! When we magnify God, we magnify faith, and our problems shrink. No matter what we experience, we can be confident in God's Word. He always keeps His promises! Jeremiah 1:12 says:

Then the Lord said to me…"I am ready to perform My word."

NKJV

…I am watching to see that my word is fulfilled.

NIV

Then said the Lord to me…"I am alert and active, watching over My word to perform it."

AMP

For He performs what is appointed for me, And many such things are with Him.

Job 23:14

As believers, we are all a part of this great adventure. Not everyone is called to the five-fold ministry, but all are called to be the hands and feet of Jesus and represent Him to the uttermost parts of the earth. God is not holding out on us. If we desire to see lives changed through the preaching of the Gospel with signs and wonders following, then let's go! Let's join the Great Adventure!

> Heal the sick, cleanse the lepers, raise the dead, cast out demons. Freely you have received, freely give.
>
> Matthew 10:8

Change your confession, change your life!

Start speaking out who God says you are today!

I am _____ (your name).

I am a party waiting to happen (1 Peter 1:8)!

Angels rejoice over me, demons flee from me (James 4:7), and God himself dances over me with singing (Zephaniah 3:17).

I am the bearer of good news (Isaiah 52:7), a minister of reconciliation (2 Corinthians 5:18), the carrier of the King of Glory (Colossians 1:27).

I am the righteousness of Christ (2 Corinthians 5:21) and a temple of the Holy Spirit (1 Corinthians 6:19).

I have an unction from the Holy One, and I know all things (1 John 2:20).

I have the mind of Christ (1 Corinthians 2:16), I am anointed by God (1 John 2:27), and I was created by Him for good works (Ephesians 2:10).

I have favor with God, favor with man, and a good understanding (Luke 2:52).

I am chosen by God (John 15:16, Ephesians 1:4), I have been sanctified (1 Corinthians 6:11) and made truly Holy. As Jesus is, so am I in this world (1 John 4:17).

I am always on God's mind; He thinks about me constantly (Psalm 139:17-18). Even before the creation of the world, I was planned (Ephesians 1:4). I am a child of the King, adopted into His family (Ephesians 1:5), an heir in Christ (Romans 8:17), and accepted in the Beloved (Ephesians 1:6).

I am blessed with every spiritual blessing in heavenly places (Ephesians 1:3). I lack no good thing (Psalm 34:10). I have an abundance for every good work (2 Corinthians 9:8). I was pre-destined by God for success (Romans 8:28-30).

I am placed and seated with Christ, a king and priest, part of a chosen generation, a peculiar people (1 Peter 2:9).

I am blessed coming in and going out (Deuteronomy 28:6). My family is blessed, my flocks are blessed (Deuteronomy 28:4), and everything I touch prospers (Deuteronomy 28:8). I am the head and not the tail, above the circumstances and not beneath them (Deuteronomy 28:13).

No weapon formed against me can prosper (Isaiah 54:17), no plague can come near my dwelling—my house or my body (Psalm 91:10), and nothing can separate me from the love of God—not angels or demons, not principalities or powers, nothing in this world or out of it (Romans 8:38-39).

I am equipped with the full armor of God (Ephesians 6:13), packed full of the Holy Spirit with more than enough power inside of me to raise the dead (Romans 8:11), heal the sick, and cast out devils (Matthew 10:1).

My faith can move mountains (Mark 11:23), my words contain life and death (Proverbs 18:21), my life was bought at a price. Jesus covered it (1 Corinthians 6:20).

My days are appointed (Psalm 139:16). My life is protected (Mark 16:18). Angels encamp around me (Psalm 34:7), and the blessings of God encircle me (Psalm 103:4), go before me, and overtake me (Deuteronomy 28:2).

The Creator of the universe, my Dad, loves me with an everlasting love (Jeremiah 31:3). He is with me always (Hebrews 13:5). He thinks about me constantly (Psalm 139:17). He knows everything about me, even the number of hairs on my head (Matthew 10:30). His love for me is inescapable, insurmountable, and irrefutable.

I am all around awesome; just ask my Dad!

PRAYER OF SALVATION

God loves you—no matter who you are, no matter what your past. God loves you so much that he gave his one and only begotten Son for you. The Bible tells us that "... whoever believes in him shall not perish but have eternal life" (John 3:16 NIV). Jesus laid down His life and rose again so that we could spend eternity with Him and experience His absolute best on earth. If you would like to receive Jesus into your life, say the following prayer out loud and mean it in your heart.

Heavenly Father, I come to you admitting that I am a sinner. Right now, I choose to turn away from sin, and I ask you to cleanse me of all unrighteousness. I believe that Your son, Jesus, died on the cross to take away my sins. I also believe that he rose again from the dead so that I might be forgiven of my sins and made righteous through faith in him. I call upon the name of Jesus Christ to be the Savior and Lord of my life. Jesus, I choose to follow You and ask You that You fill me with the power of the Holy Spirit. I declare that right now I am a child of God. I am free from sin and full of the righteousness of God. I am saved in Jesus' name. Amen.

If you prayed this prayer to receive Jesus Christ as your Savior for the first time, please contact us to receive a free book by writing to us.

www.harrisonhouse.com

The Harrison House Vision

Proclaiming the truth and the power

Of the Gospel of Jesus Christ

With excellence;

Challenging Christians to

Live victoriously,

Grow spiritually,

Know God intimately.